"Just enough information for you to enjoy the great pleasure of wine."

THE INSTANT
WINE
CONNOISSEUR

Second Edition

A practical guide to tasting, buying and cooking with wine

Including recipes and wine pairings by great chefs.

Mervyn L. Hecht
With recipes and food comments by
Judy Lamm

Invinoveritas Publishing Company
Los Angeles, CA

Published by Invinoveritas Publishing Company
311 Amalfi Drive, Santa Monica, California 90402

Cover design by Pearl & Associates, Inc.
Manufactured in the United States of America

Hecht, Mervyn and Lamm, Judy
The Instant Wine Connoisseur:
A Practical Guide to Tasting, Buying and Cooking With Wine

Design coordination and printing supervision by
Top Floor Publications

1. Wine and wine making. 2. Cookery—Wine. I. Title

ISBN 0-9662481-5-5

Printed in Hong Kong

CONTENTS

Introduction

QUESTIONS YOU SHOULD ASK

This is a book about the tastes of wines. The object of the book is to help you, the wine drinker, identify and remember the most important wines, so that wine labels and wine lists begin to make some sense. But I'm not trying to write a book that requires you to have to study and memorize in order to understand and remember wines. Because people don't want to do that, most wine drinkers are lost when reading a wine list or looking at a wine label. So what I do in this book is explain about taste and how to do it, then lead you into tasting the differences among the major wines. By focusing only on the most important wines and how they taste, I hope to avoid cluttering up your mind with more information than you need. In other words, I hope to impart a methodology, and just enough information to get started, for you to enjoy the great pleasures of wine.

In addition, I discuss in the book what I think are the most important aspects of wine customs, such as which wines to drink with which foods, which wines to decant, which wines to age, and how. Finally, I briefly discuss general health concerns about drinking wine—in fact, is it good for us at well as delightful?

To accomplish these goals I believe that the prospective wine drinker will need to have a few questions answered, such as the following:

QUESTION 1:

WHY ANOTHER BOOK ABOUT WINES?

Every month I get a book by mail that is nothing more than a long list of wine books. There must be hundreds listed, and there are many books in print that are not listed. Just this month I myself bought three books about wine, and what wonderful works they are! But two of them are really big, and are going to take a long time for me to read. I'll enjoy every minute of it.

One of these two books reads more like a novel; it's a history of the Zinfandel grape in California. By the time I've read this book I'll probably know more about the history of Zinfandel than I do about my own family's history.

As interesting as these books are, none of them focuses on the practical problems that most wine drinkers face, such as:

— How do the wines on a restaurant wine list (or in a store) taste, and how can I remember the tastes?

— When ordering wine in a restaurant, which wine should I order, and what factors should I take into consideration?

— Which wines match well with which foods?

— What are reasonable prices for various wines?

— What should I know about storing and serving wine?

— Is wine good for you—or is it harmful?

These are the issues that most wine drinkers face. So while production methods and Chateau history make for interesting reading, as a practical matter they don't help us to be able to look at a wine list in a restaurant and imagine the taste of the wines listed so that we can decide which one to order. Certainly that's what we do with the food on the menu: we think about the taste of salmon, or beef, and choose one or the other. You probably can remember what salmon tasted like the last time you ate it. Remembering the taste of wine is much more difficult for most people, and as a result they order wine based on color (red or white) and price.

It is not clear why there is such a difference between ordering from the food menu, and ordering from the wine list. It's not that there are more wines than foods. I read somewhere that there are dozens of types of shrimp, and I know there are lots of varieties of apples. But when I see a shrimp dish listed on the menu, or an apple dessert, I have some idea what they are going to taste like. That's because there is an apple taste and a shrimp taste, and I remember them. And like most people, even though there is a difference in taste between apples, I generally remember which ones are more crisp and tart, and which more soft and sweet.

The problem for the wine drinker is, I believe, that the bottle doesn't say on the label anything that is the equivalent of "apple" or "shrimp." While some great connoisseurs may be able to identify a particular "Chateau Margaux taste," I can only tell that it's probably a Bordeaux. And even then I might be wrong, and it might turn out to be a California Cabernet Sauvignon that's been blended in the Bordeaux manner. But because both of those wines are made primarily from the Cabernet Sauvignon grape, they have similar tastes.

Since particular grapes do have a distinctive taste, if you know what grape or blend of grapes a wine is made from, it helps to anticipate what it will taste like.

Yes, there are differences between vineyards, producers, years (vintages), and geography. But there is a "Cabernet Sauvignon taste," and generally I can identify it when I taste it. In other words, to focus the mind on the taste of a wine, I need to know the taste of the primary grape from which the wine is made. For example, it's difficult to distinguish a Barolo from a Barbaresco, because both are made from the same grape, but it's not hard to tell either of those wines from a Chianti, which is made from a different grape.

So I decided to write a book that describes, in SIMPLE terms, the tastes of the primary wine grapes, and the wines we see most often on wine lists and in wine stores. And I decided NOT to include a lot of information about the climate, the soil, the production processes, and all the other information that makes other peoples' books such interesting reading. Instead, I include just a few interesting facts about only the most important grapes—just enough so that something about each important grape stays in the mind.

Nor do I attempt in this book to discuss every grape from which wines are made—or even most of them. There are hundreds, (thousands?), of wine grapes, and that is one reason why it is difficult to buy wine or order it from a wine list: there are too many, with too many confusing names. My goal in this book is to select the most important grapes — those from which the most important wines are made that we customarily drink with food. My hope is that armed with this information, you will be able to find a few wines on each wine list with familiar names that you can associate with a particular taste.

Only then does it make sense to move on to evaluate the year, the producer, and the price, from which a more discriminating decision can be made when buying a bottle or ordering wine with dinner. In other words, if you can mentally taste the wine, you can tell how much you are going to like it, and mentally pair it with the food you plan to eat. Then you can evaluate the price, to see if it is reasonable, in light of the reputation of the producer and the vintage.

In addition to the problem of connecting the visual sense (reading the list or label) to an anticipated taste, there are a lot of social conventions, "snobbery," and folklore about wine that makes many drinkers wary of doing something gauche. Does veal require red or white wine? Should Port be served before or after dinner? Should a 1982 Chateauneuf-du-Pape be decanted or served from the bottle?

These are some of the practical questions I hope to answer in this book.

QUESTION 2:
WHAT DO I NEED TO KNOW TO INTELLIGENTLY BUY A BOTTLE OF WINE?

The first thing you should want to know is "What is it going to taste like?" In order to get to that point I discovered that you have to understand a little bit about the physiology of tasting: how the tongue, eye, nose ,brain AND MIND work together to create a "taste." As I explain more completely below, some of what we taste is from the tastebuds on the tongue, most is from sensors in the nose, and a bit is added by the mind from what we see, and what we know from current information and prior experience.

Secondly, you might want to know what special conventions are generally recommended to enjoy wine, and which wines traditionally go with what foods. A few recipes that use wine for flavor will help in this connection.

Finally, more and more wine drinkers are asking health related questions about wine. For example, one common question is "should I drink wine if I'm taking antibiotics?" There are a number of medical conditions, such as diabetes and liver conditions, that raise questions about the good sense of drinking wine. My wife keeps telling me that I drink too much, my friend the pathologist tells me that autopsies on drunks reveal extraordinarily clear arteries, and I read in my newspaper that French people who drink red wine have less heart disease, in spite of a high cholesterol diet. What is the latest medical information on drinking wine, and how should we apply it to our lives?

QUESTION 3:

WHY ALL THIS FUSS
ABOUT WINE ANYWAY?

For me, that's the most interesting question of all. Grapes are the number one agricultural crop in California. About 100 BILLION dollars worth of grapes are sold on the wholesale market worldwide each year. People have been drinking wine for more than 5000 years. Noah planted a vineyard 4000 years ago, produced some wine, and got drunk from it. More time, money, and land are devoted to wine than to either sex or religion! WHY? I have a few ideas, and I'll share them with you below.

Port Grimaud, France, September, 2001

Taste

SECTION ONE:

THE HOW

Taste is a subjective experience. For this reason we can never be sure it's the same for me as it is for you. In fact, we can be sure that some tastes will give me more pleasure than they will for you, and vice versa. But because of our common taste experiences and common language we can communicate the similarities and differences, and thereby increase our understanding. To have the common experiences, however, requires that each of us have some memory bank of tastes from which to draw. As a result of common experiences and communication, objective standards begin to mold the subjectivity of individual views. In other words, interaction with other people has an effect on our reaction to the subjective taste of wine, and can give it more meaning and enjoyment.

Let me give you an example. Years ago certain producers in Greece stored their wines in barrels made from wood that gave the wine the taste of the resin in the wood. For many people the flavor of resin, which is a bit like turpentine, is very off-putting in a wine. But lots of Greek wine drinkers in that region got used to the flavor, and began to look forward to it. Over time, other people began to associate that flavor in wine with certain Greek foods. Today if a French wine tasted of resin it would be sent back. But retsina from Greece is sold all over the world, and many of us enjoy it with Greek food. The common experience of drinking wine with that particular flavor, eventually disseminated to others, created a new objective standard, or expectation in our memory bank, for the taste of resin with Greek food.

Because taste is experiential, it is best if these "common experiences" arise by actually tasting the wine. No matter how many books we read, we can't learn to ride a bicycle or hit a golf drive well until we do it a few times. Even if I tell you that the taste of resin in wine goes well with Greek food, you're not going to like it unless you drink it a few times with Greek food—any more than you liked spinach the first time your mother told you it was good for you, or the first time a Japanese friend offered me some sea urchin sushi!

In fact, to create such a memory bank requires not only that we have the experience, but that we focus our attention on it in special ways. If each of us walks past a shoe store every day for a year, but we don't notice it, the experience will not create a useful memory. Focus—or attention—is the first step.

For this reason, when tasting wine, certain rituals have become customary. If you follow them your attention will be focused on the elements of taste, and those elements will begin to stick in your mind.

A typical list of rules to follow to taste, evaluate, and commit tastes to memory is as follows:

1. Clear your palate and taste buds with a glass of water. Pour some wine into a bowl shaped glass, but fill the glass only one-third full, to leave enough room in the glass for the aroma of the wine to gather. The wine should be slightly cooler than room temperature. Some people like white wine as cool as 50 degrees.

2. LOOK at the wine, preferably with a white background, and make a mental note of the color. Note both the color at the center, and the color at the edges. Older red wine tends to turn orange or brown at the edges. Certain white wines tend to pale at the edges. In addition to the color, note the clarity (or dullness or cloudiness) of the wine, to make sure it is well made and not spoiled. Finally, look at the viscosity, or body (from a visual point of view) to anticipate the feel of the liquid on the tongue.

3. SMELL the wine, and verbalize your reaction. Verbalizing makes it easier to remember. Since our vocabulary doesn't really contain precise words for the odors of wine, it is necessary to use words that are analogous to the odors of the wine, such as floral, fruity, chocolate, earthy, etc. No wine tastes like chocolate, but there are flavors in some wines that are reminiscent of chocolate. The smell of wine is referred to professionally as its "NOSE," or "bouquet." Experts separate the various smells into two categories, one based on the smell of the grape, and the other based on the aging characteristics of the wine, such as oak, or the special bouquet derived from long aging in the bottle.

4. SWIRL the wine and smell it again. We do this because aeration sometimes affects the nose of the wine.

5. SIP some of the wine into the mouth with air, then let it run over the tongue. Pay attention to the first tastes. The chemical contact of the wine on the various tongue sensors (sweet, sour, salty and bitter) combines with the nose to create a first taste. While it used to be thought that only the four primary tastes came from the tongue, recent scientific studies on the taste buds of eels (which apparently have very large taste buds, and are easier to study) have shown that the combinations of tastes in the mouth create a much greater variety of tastes than originally thought possible. This first taste of wine is sometimes referred to by professionals as its "entry."

6. Swirl the wine in the mouth, then SWALLOW it. Note the change in taste from the first taste, and pay attention to the differences in the aftertaste, and the duration and strength of the aftertaste. Wine with more intense fruit and adequate acidity will have a stronger and longer aftertaste, enhancing the pleasure of the wine. The taste the wine leaves in the mouth after swallowing it (or spitting it out, in a professional tasting) is what we refer to as the "aftertaste." The aftertaste is very important in tasting wines, food and drink in general.

7. Think and TALK about the taste, paying attention to at least the following six elements:

— (a) How intense is the flavor.

— (b) Is the wine sweet, medium, or dry; ("dry" refers to a lack of sweetness).

— (c) How tart is the wine. Tartness is caused by acidity, and is very prized in some wines. Think of orange juice, and how good the tart taste is with the fruit flavor.

— (d) How astringent is the wine; astringency is usually found in red wines known for long life, and is a result of tannin from grape skins. Young full bodied wines are often more tannic in the first few years, then the tannins soften. Coffee and tea have a tannic taste that many people like.

21

— (e) Is the wine balanced? The most pleasing wines have a balance between the elements described above. The proportions, however, are a subjective matter in which preference varies widely among wine lovers.

— (f) Finally, what is the impression of aftertaste, the taste that remains after swallowing? A pleasant lingering flavor is one of the pleasures of fine wines.

So far we've been talking about the taste of wine. But all of this applies to food and drink in general. One of the benefits of learning to appreciate the taste of wine is that it enhances our appreciation of foods and beverages. For example, try the procedure above with orange juice. When I did it recently I discovered that the orange juice had a fruity, sweet nose, but with less orange to it than I had expected. The first taste was of orange, but the aftertaste was long and tart, with a flavor I connect more with pineapple than with orange. I was surprised at the acidity on the tongue, and how reminiscent it was of the aftertaste of a white wine that is high in acid. On another occasion I noticed how much sweeter this orange juice was than the last one I had drunk.

If you begin to focus your attention on taste, you will be surprised how quickly you can begin to identify the major spices in foods, such as onion, thyme, cinnamon, basil, tarragon, etc. And practicing on foods is good practice for wine. The fact is that an appreciation of taste in general makes dining more pleasurable, and helps us to eat more slowly and to eat less, without any reduction of pleasure.

SECTION TWO:

THE WHY

My mother used to say that it's easier to follow rules if you understand the reasons behind them. So why do we look at the color, swirl the wine in the glass, smell first, and talk afterward?

Taste is a very complex activity involving sight, sound, texture, taste buds, mouth sensors, memory, and—above all—smell. Let's briefly examine each of these elements:

1. For wine tasting, sound is the least important part. Some people don't like crunchy foods, and soft versus hard can be determined partly by sound. Since all wine is liquid the sound doesn't vary enough to be a factor.

2. Texture is part of what the mouth sensors sense. The thickness of a liquid, called viscosity, plays a small part in wine tasting. Some wines are sensed as thicker, or more viscous, than others. This is associated with the "body" of the wine, although not necessarily with the strength of the flavor. Wines with more viscosity, or body, are usually perceived as being "richer" tasting, because more viscosity is usually associated with more extract, and thus stronger flavor.

   Viscosity is usually tested by wine drinkers by swirling the wine in the glass, and then looking at the "legs," the wine that runs down the inside of the glass after swirling. The existence of "legs" is an indication of a viscous wine, a wine that will be expected to have a full bodied texture.

   Viscosity plays a minor part in wine tasting. The small part it does play is confounded or reinforced by what we see. Wines from southern, hotter regions tend toward more viscosity, while wines from the northern, cooler climates tend toward "thinness."

3. Sight is often a major confound in taste. Some kids won't eat spinach because of its appearance, not because of its taste. Dark brown foods are often considered unappetizing, as are meats dripping blood. Without looking first, some people can't tell a red wine from a white wine. People used to drinking mild rosé are often surprised when they taste a strong flavored rosé.

23

Sight is helpful in tasting as an aid to memory. The visual analysis of the color and viscosity of the wine bring forth memories of similar wines from the past, and prepares the mouth and the taste buds for the pleasure to come, much as Pavlov's bell prepared his dog's taste buds for dinner. Appreciation of color and associations from memory are part of the pleasure of wine.

4. By and large, it's the combination of tongue sensors and smell that creates the unique taste of wine. The smell sensors in the nose are more important than the tongue's sensors, although these are among the least understood of our senses. When we swallow a liquid, some of the molecules of the liquid are forced up into the nasal passages, where they trigger a signal directly to the limbic system in the brain, the seat of emotions, sexuality, memory and drive.

While not well understood from a physiological point of view, the significance of smell is well known. From an evolutionary point of view smell has great significance. It is the oldest sense and has the most direct access to the brain of any of our senses. Certainly smell was involved in sexual selection and in the testing of food and drink before eating or drinking. Even now perfume manufacturers would have us believe that the right smell will create sexual interest in others. And my wife insists on smelling any suspect food before eating it, "just to be sure it's safe."

Don't underestimate the power of our noses. I read somewhere that sharks can smell blood when there is one part in several million in water. That's only slightly better than some wine tasters who, after a taste, can tell the year and maker of the wine. Through smell, a baby finds its mother's breast, and a mother can identify her baby in the dark. In fact, one percent of all our genes are devoted to detecting odors, and this is the largest gene family we know of in mammals. According to nature, smell is our most important method of contact with the outside world! 1

But because sight and touch have become more important in today's world (certainly in sexual selection) we've neglected the power of our sense of smell, and most of us haven't developed it. Even without paying special attention to it, however, the average person can identify over 10,000 odors, and can detect them from a very small source; my wife can spot someone smoking on an airplane 15 rows away, with her eyes closed.

An interest in wine gives us the opportunity to develop our sense of smell, and permits us to enter into a world of different and primitive sensual perception. And alcohol is one of a small number of substances (like hot peppers) that excite certain nerves which contribute to the enjoyment of food, particularly as we age.

5. Finally, it's time to talk about the brain, because that's where all this sensory information is processed. Looking at the wine, smelling it, swirling it around the mouth, and then letting it roll around on the tongue before drinking it gives all of the useful sensors a chance to send clues about the wine to the brain. This enhances our analysis, and, in appropriate cases, our enjoyment of the wine.

    Interestingly, there are two separate ways in which the brain influences our analysis of taste. The nasal sensors go directly to that part of the brain which is involved in memory and emotion. This is thought to be why certain smells create sexual desire, and others remind us of events in our childhood. At the other extreme, data from the visual sensors (our eyes) is heavily processed before the data gets to the brain, then processed in non-intuitive, complex ways in various areas of the brain: color is sensed in one area, shape in another, movement in a third, etc. One of the reasons that taste is such a complex subject is that it is created by a combination of data from tongue sensors, mouth sensors, nasal sensors, eyes, subjective experiences, memory, and analytic processes, all of which are processed differently by the brain, and then combined to create the experience of taste.

Having these techniques in mind, it's time to try wine made from each of the major grapes.

1 If you're interested in the complexity of smell, read the wonderful article by Professor Richard Axel, The Molecular Logic of Smell, October 1995 Scientific American Magazine.

Red Wines

FRANCE, CALIFORNIA, OREGON AND WASHINGTON

There are far too many red wine grapes grown in France to be of interest to someone who just wants to enjoy wine with dinner. Just to spell some of them can create a controversy among the French. Of all these grapes, the most famous red wines are made from just five grapes, and I will discuss a sixth grape just because I like it, and a lot of French wine is made from it.

The same grapes that are famous in France are the ones most famous in California, Oregon and Washington, so it only makes sense to discuss them together. And then there is California Zinfandel!

CABERNET SAUVIGNON— FROM BORDEAUX AND CALIFORNIA

Cabernet Sauvignon is the major red wine grape in the world for quality red wine, and it is grown throughout the world. It's a dark, small grape that makes a dark, tannic, strong, long-lasting wine that is said to have a nose and taste reminiscent of black currants and cedarwood. Different climates and soil have a significant effect on the flavor of the grape, so there is no substitute for trying to remember the region from which the wine comes. There is so much Cabernet sauvignon wine—pure and mixed—on the market that you just must buy a few bottles and try them together in a wine tasting to see the differences, and decide which you prefer. Excellent Cabernet is made in Napa Valley, Chile, and Australia, as well as Bordeaux. Cabernet wines made in cooler regions than those mentioned above may have a less pleasant flavor.

The most famous wines of France are made in Bordeaux, an area on the west coast of France. The traditional Bordeaux wine is a blend of three or four grapes, Cabernet Sauvignon (approximately 60%), Merlot (approximately 30%) Cabernet franc (approximately 5-10%), and Petit Verdot (5-10%). The percentages vary from year to year and from Chateau to Chateau, depending on several factors: how well each crop of grapes does, what vines were planted at each Chateau, and the mix of flavors and tannins desired. The blender tries to meld the grape flavor of the Cabernet, the softness of the Merlot, and the structure of the Cabernet Franc. Others say that in many years, Cabernet by itself is just too tannic, too dark, and too dense, and it has to be watered down with juice that is lighter and more floral. Since Merlot and Cabernet Franc meet these requirements, by planting some of each of these vines, the producer can always be sure that one or the other of these vines will be available for blending each year.

Much wine is still blended from these grapes, but there has been a trend, (particularly in California), to produce wines from a single variety of grape. So one presently finds a lot of wine that is made from 100% Cabernet Sauvignon, or 100% Merlot.

By and large, Cabernet Sauvignon benefits from a few years of aging in the bottle. The great Bordeaux wines, of course, improve after many years in the bottle, but typically Bordeaux starts to decline anywhere from five to 10 years after bottling. The price range of Bordeaux wines can vary greatly, from $4-$100 or more. The range for California Cabernet wines is a bit more narrow, but can still range from the low priced wines in the six-10 dollar range, to the premium Bordeaux style wines, such as Phelps Insignia and Opus 1 at $50-100 per bottle.

Josiah Citrin, Chef-Owner of Melisse, one of the Zagat Survey's most popular restaurants, and probably the epitome of French-California restaurants favors:

"CÔTE DE BOEUF"
WITH FINGERLING POTATOES,
A ROASTED SHALLOT AND BONE
MARROW FLAN
AND NATURAL JUS

to be paired with Cheval Blanc Wine
(Serves 2)

31

CÔTE DE BOEUF:

1 each	*18-20 oz. bone in prime rib steak*
12 each	*fingerling potatoes (slice at an angle 1/2" thick)*
7 each	*whole garlic cloves*
1 tsp	*chopped thyme*
1 each	*shallot, finely diced*
1 tsp	*chopped parsley*
to taste	*sea salt and crushed 5 peppercorn mix (green, red, black, white, coriander)*
4 T	*unsalted butter*
3/4 cup	*red wine*
1/2 cup	*veal stock or chicken stock*
1 each	*shallot, sliced*
2 each	*sprigs of thyme*
1 each	*bayleaf*
	oil for cooking

Roasted Shallot and Bone Marrow Flan: *Makes 5 - 1/4 cup flan molds*

1/4 cup	*heavy cream*
1/4 cup	*milk*
2 each	*large eggs*
3 ounces	*bone marrow*
3 each	*shallots roasted in oil until tender (do not let brown)*
to taste	*salt and white pepper*
	pan coating spray

Prepare Flans: Heat oven to 300 degrees. Spray flan molds and set aside. Combine the milk and cream in a small pot and bring to a boil. Remove from heat and set aside. Bring water to a boil in a small pot. Add the bone marrow and simmer until very tender, about 10 minutes. Transfer to a blender with a slotted spoon, add the roasted shallot and puree until smooth. Transfer to a food processor and add scalded milk and cream, the egg, salt and pepper. Strain through a chinois.

Pour the strained liquid into the prepared molds and place in a small baking pan. Add boiling water (enough to come 3/4 of the way up the mold). Bake uncovered in the oven for 45 minutes. To test doneness, after 40 minutes remove a flan, loosen sides with a knife and invert flan onto a plate. If done, the flan will stand up and hold its shape. When cut in half, the center will be solid. Remove flans from oven and let sit in hot water for 10 to 30 minutes.

Prepare Fingerling Potatoes: Heat oven to 400 degrees. Heat a large non-stick sauté pan over high heat. Add oil and potatoes and sauté for 3 minutes, mixing often. Add five garlic cloves and continue cooking until slightly golden. Add 1 tbl. butter and chopped thyme. Cook in the oven 4 more minutes. Total cooking time is about 12 minutes. Remove from oven and keep warm.

Final preparation: When the flans have finished baking, cook de "cote de boeuf". Heat 3 tbl. of oil on a heavy skillet over high heat. Meanwhile, season the steak on both sides with sea salt and paper mix. Add steak to the skillet and cook for about 3 minutes per side. Place in oven and cook for another 8 minutes for medium rare. Take out and let rest in a warm place for at least 10 minutes, but no longer than 15. In the same pan, cook one clove of garlic and the sliced shallot. Deglaze with red wine, add thyme and bay leaf and reduce until almost dry. Add veal stock and reduce by 1/2. Fold in 1 tbl. butter, season to taste, strain and keep warm. Reheat potatoes and add chopped parsley, salt and paper.

Presentation: Heat a large platter. Unmold flans, arrange potatoes nicely, carve the meat from the bone and slice it against the grain. Fan the meat and nap with the sauce. Sprinkle meat with coarse sea salt and serve immediately.

One of the Rollet Estates in Boreaux

THE MERLOT GRAPES OF
CALIFORNIA AND BORDEAUX

Traditionally, the Merlot grape is used for blending. It is sort of a fluke that there is one Chateau in Bordeaux, Chateau Petrus, that makes a 100% Merlot wine, and it has become the most expensive red wine in the world! Partly because of this, and partly because the grape is easier to grow, there has been a trend, particularly in California, to produce 100% Merlot wine. It is less tannic than Cabernet, slightly sweeter (less dry), and is ready to drink at an earlier age.

When Merlot vines are allowed to overproduce grapes, the wine comes out tasteless, particularly in northern climates. But Washington state produces some good Merlot, as does California from Napa Valley south to Santa Barbara. The prime site for Merlot is still the Pomerol region of Bordeaux, and the major use of Merlot is still for blending with Cabernet Sauvignon.

Merlot wines age less well, and—with the exception of the few great Bordeaux estates known for this grape—sell in the range of $6-$22 both in France and in California.

Roger Belland and his Burgandy Cellar

THE PINOT NOIR GRAPES OF BURGUNDY AND OREGON

The next great grape of France (after Cabernet Sauvignon) is the Pinot Noir grape of the Burgundy region, with the state of Oregon fast on its heels trying to match the popularity of the great Burgundy wines. The Pinot Noir grape is the most difficult to grow, and the wines produced from it vary the greatest in quality and taste. In addition to these factors, some varieties of the vine (called "clones") produce inferior grapes which are also called Pinot Noir. Another problem is that some of the producers take short-cuts which produce inferior wines.

By and large, great wines from the Pinot Noir grape come from a small area in the Burgundy region of France. Because the wine is so highly prized, this region has been broken down into many small vineyards, each of which produces its own wine in its own way.

Pinot Noir and similar varieties are grown in many places in the world. However, the great burgundies, which are among the most sought after and among the most expensive wines in the world, have a complexity and beauty of taste that have never been matched anywhere else. A lot of the grapes grown are used in champagnes, but it is the long-lived, silky tasting red wines that have made this grape famous for over 2000 years. The characteristic flavor comparisons are black cherry, raspberry, rose petal, earth, herbs, and spices. In lesser Pinot Noir wines the flavor of lighter cherries predominates.

The great Burgundy wines have a special complexity of flavor and mouth sensations that are beyond the power of the written word. I've tasted hints of these in some of the less expensive French Burgundy wines, and some of the better Pinot Noir wines of Oregon and California. A small producer in France once told me that part of the allure for him of the wine was that the nose reminded him of the odors when he makes love. Whether or not that is your reaction, the fact is that it's a special flavor and texture, and to produce it requires a lot of skill and effort. For that reason a really good bottle of burgundy now costs between $50 to $150. Add to that the fact that it's very difficult to tell if a bottle is going to be special or not, especially given the large number of producers, many of which have similarly confusing names, and you can begin to see why this is not a wine we drink very often.

Wines from the Pinot Noir grape do not improve with age as well as those from Cabernet Sauvignon, and only the very great Burgundy wines age well for 8 years or more.

Domaine des Tourelles in the Rhone Valley

THE OTHER RED GRAPES OF FRANCE: GRENACHE, GAMAY AND SYRAH

GRENACHE

The Grenache grape is one of the "workhorses" of French vineyards, and probably the most famous grape planted in Spain (which produces more wine than any country in the world). A lot of it is planted, and a lot of very different wines are made from it. It is almost always blended with other grapes. A lot of wonderful rosé is made from Grenache. But the most prized red wines from Grenache are the wines of the southern Rhone river valley in France. One of the most famous of these is Chateauneuf du Pape, which comes from a small city near Avignon in the south of France.

In the southern Rhone valley wines in general are called "Côtes du Rhone," which just means that the vines are grown on the coasts, or banks, of the Rhone river. Wines of higher quality are given the names of cities or villages. Each village boasts of the particular taste its soil gives to the grapes, and—historically—the mix of grapes varied from village to village. While the wines of this region are primarily made from Grenache, as many as another dozen or so grape varieties are blended with the Grenache, according to tradition and production variations from year to year.

Chateauneuf du Pape (which translates to "the Pope's new castle"— the Popes used to live in Avignon before moving to the Vatican) is one such village. Gigondas and Lirac are other well known villages with excellent wines.

Most Côtes du Rhone wines are a medium light garnet in color, with a fruity flavor suggesting a wine that is ready to drink when young, and not likely to improve after two to three years in the bottle. The better wines, such as Chateauneuf du Pape made from the better producers, are darker in color, age for 6-10 years —or more in special years, and have a special Grenache flavor that is quite unlike Bordeaux or Burgundy, or any other grape or fruit. As I've said before, Bordeaux often reminds me of dark raspberries, and Burgundy often reminds me of cherries; but the taste of Grenache doesn't remind me of anything else. Like a mango, it has its own distinctive flavor, and thus it is easier to identify than many other grapes. Sometimes the nose reminds me of flowers, sometimes roses.

One of the best features of southern Rhone wines is their price. Mainly through historical accident the wines of this region never experienced the rush of price increases brought on by heavy export trade. A good Côte du Rhone can still be purchased for six to eight dollars, and some of the best village named production can be found for $12-18. In the best years, even the best of the Chateauneuf du Pape costs between $35-80, significantly less than the great Bordeaux, and half or one-fourth the price of the great Burgundies.

Rhone style wines (typically called "Syrah" or "Grenache") are in vogue among a group of growers in California, (sometimes referred to as the "Rhone Rangers). Here great strides are allegedly being made to improve the traditional Rhone grape varieties. Results vary.

Joe Miller of Joe's Restaurant in Venice, which is consistently on the top 10 in the Zagat Guide for Los Angeles, favors the Australian wine Trevor Jones' "Boots Red," which is an Australian Barossa Valley Grenache, with Hazelnut Crusted Goat Cheese with Roasted Beets, Micro Greens and Hazelnut Oil. Joe will soon be coming out with a new cookbook:

HAZELNUT CRUSTED GOAT CHEESE WITH ROASTED BEETS, MICRO GREENS AND HAZELNUT OIL

Recipe by Judy Lamm

INGREDIENTS

Salad Dressing:

1	shallot, minced
pinch	dry mustard
1/8 tsp each	fresh ground pepper and salt
1 tsp	minced fresh tarragon or chervil
1/4 cup	Sherry wine vinegar
1/4 cup	hazelnut oil

METHOD

1. Mix all ingredients well.

For Beets:

> 2   medium-large fresh beets
> 1 T   hazelnut oil

Aluminum foil or small pan with lid

METHOD

1. Wash and dry beets. Put into foil or into oven-proof small pan with lid. Sprinkle with oil.
2. Bake for 45 minutes to 1 hour at 375 degrees F or until slightly soft. Remove from oven, peel and dice. Sprinkle with some salad dressing.

For Greens:

> 2 cups   micro greens

METHOD

1. Wash and dry greens. Toss with dressing. Divide greens between 4 plates. Top with roasted beets.

For Goat Cheese:

> 12 slices   goat cheese about 3/8" thick
> 1/2 cup   toasted peeled, minced hazelnuts

METHOD

1. Dip goat cheese into hazelnuts to coat. Either place on cookie sheet and heat in 350 degree F oven 3 to 5 minutes or heat in non-stick frying pan.
2. Top each plate with 3 slices of goat cheese and serve immediately.

TO PREPARE IN A.M.: Make salad dressing and beets. Wash greens. Toast and mince nuts.

TO PREPARE A DAY IN ADVANCE: Make salad dressing and beets. Wash greens, wrap in a towel and refrigerate. Toast and mince nuts and store in a tightly sealed container.

TO FREEZE: No

GAMAY

This grape is famous for only one reason: it is the basis of Beaujolais, one of the most popular wines in the world. Almost all the vines planted in the Beaujolais region of France (located between Champagne and the Rhone valley) are Gamay.

Like the southern Rhone valley, there is plain Beaujolais, often called Beaujolais Village (technically one step up in quality from the bottom) and special Beaujolais which is given the name of one of the villages in Beaujolais. And so some Beaujolais fans prefer Moulin-a-Vent, some prefer Morgon, and others favor Beaujolais from other villages.

Beaujolais is just the opposite of what we think of in fine wines. No one puts it aside to age. Good Beaujolais is inexpensive, light, fruity, not complex, young, and ready to drink. In fact, it's now in vogue to drink it as soon as possible after it's produced, before it gets any bottle age at all. Beaujolais parties are the rage in Paris, right after the wine is bottled, and the fresh young Beaujolais Nouveau is flown to New York and other cities around the world where eager wine buffs celebrate the Beaujolais harvest with Beaujolais parties. Prices range from $4 to $12.

Wine Makers in the Southern Rhone Valley.

THE SYRAH GRAPE:

HERMITAGE, CROZES-HERMITAGE, AND CORNAS WINES

This is the vine brought by the Greeks from Persia to Gaul, where it was planted first near Marseilles, then up the Rhone river, and finally on a hillside near the Town of Tain-Hermitage, just south of Lyon, France, where it has flourished for over 2,300 years. Of course, the French claim it was a native vine, and that the Romans merely showed the locals how to improve it. Whichever is correct, writers at the time of Jesus praised the wines from that famous hill, and were impressed with the length of time wine had already been produced there. Two thousand years ago, the Roman historian Pliny the Elder was so impressed by the wines from this hillside that he went to visit it-and a trip from Naples to Lyon must not have been easy in those days.

Syrah is still planted in the Languedoc, a region near Marseilles, and is the basis for a number of wines from the Languedoc, where it is usually blended with Grenache and other grapes. It was transported to

Australia, where—under the name Shiraz—it has also flourished and is the basis of some excellent, long-lived red wines. A few producers grow the grape in California, where the wine from this grape comes out tasting very differently from the flavor of the wine of the same name in France. This is probably because of the differences in climate. The climate of Washington state is more like that of the Ardesch region of France, and there is some hope among wine lovers that the Syrah planted there will produce wines more like those produced in France.

In years when the weather does not result in first quality grapes, some of the French producers use the Syrah grape to make a wonderful rosé. But by and large the Syrah grape is famous for making a long-lived red wine called Hermitage, from just one small hill at the town of Tain-Hermitage. Syrah grapes from nearby areas are used to produce similar wines called Crozes-Hermitage, Cornas, St. Joseph, and a bit further north, Côte-Roti. All of these wines are made exclusively from the Syrah grape, except that Côte-Roti usually has a small amount of the Viognier grape added, a white grape with an exceptional nose that adds a floral scent to the Syrah.

The Syrah grape does not have the distinctive flavor of the Grenache grape. The taste is more variable, depending on the soil and the way the wine is made, and the wines can be light and fruity, or dark, tannic, and very month filling. The great Hermitage wines are those that are fairly dark red, with the flavors of sweet licorice, pepper, dark berries, and sometimes an earthy or leathery overtone. The entry is smooth, from aging in wood for several years, and there is a substantial after-taste. The wines are usually kept by local drinkers for six to eight years before opening. In the better years these wines reach their peak after 13-20 years or more.

Unlike Bordeaux and Burgundy, where hundreds of small producers abound, there are only a few large and a few small producers around Tain-Hermitage. And many of the grape growers sell their grapes to the local cooperative, which is one of the most technically advanced facilities in France and makes excellent wine—some of which, they claim, is then sold to the more famous producers to bottle and sell at much higher prices because these producers are well known.

The best known Syrah wines, from the hills of Tain Hermitage, sell in retail stores for $25-60. But there are many excellent Syrah wines from the Languedoc region in France, from the Rhone Valley, and from other areas of the world that sell in the six-$15 range.

CALIFORNIA ZINFANDEL

Finally we come to one of the world's great wines and great mysteries. Zinfandel is wine from a grape that has inspired an extensive following, about which many books and articles have been written, and which has been responsible for the financial success of some unlikely vineyards.

First of all, in spite of extensive genetic testing, no one is sure where the vines originated. The best current guess is Southeast Italy, but Hungary and Yugoslavia are also possibilities. However it got to California, that is where it has flourished, and that is where the prime wine from this grape is made.

First, let's dispel some confusion. One of the best selling wines in California is white Zinfandel, which I would describe as a sweet rosé. As with most rosés, white Zinfandel is made from red grapes, but without letting the skins, (which give the red color and certain of the flavors) stay in the liquid very long.

In no way would I call this a great wine, except for the financial success it has bestowed upon a number of vineyards that got on the bandwagon at the outset. Its popularity arises from the California custom of substituting a cool wine drink for a traditional aperitif. As a sweet aperitif, white Zinfandel can hit the spot.

But for purposes of this chapter (on red wines) what I mean by Zinfandel is the red wine produced by a small number of California vineyards. It is produced by some with great seriousness. None has huge production, and much of the best Zinfandel produced is allocated in advance to "friends of the vineyard" who automatically buy one or more cases every year, and to a few specialty wine stores. Much of the Zinfandel that we read about in the wine magazines is not for sale in the marketplace.

Zinfandel is a big, red wine that ages well. The nature of the grape is such that it can produce a wide range of flavors, levels of alcohol, and types of wine. When made by the six to eight serious Zinfandel makers in California it has a flavor similar to the Cabernet Sauvignon grape, but with a more spicy nose and flavor. It is less tannic than some full bodied red wine, and feels more full, or viscous, on the tongue. It tastes of dark berry, with a bit of a mild black pepper overtone. Only the berry and pepper taste of certain Zinfandels permit even the careful taster to be able to distinguish the taste of the Zinfandel from a Cabernet Sauvignon or a Merlot.

One of the best and most distinguishing features of Zinfandel is its price. For a bottle of quality similar to a $35 Bordeaux you can expect to pay eight-$18. Only a few of the very best and limited vintages sell for more than $18.

One used to see, and occasionally now finds "Late Harvest Zinfandel," a fad from the 1970's in which Zinfandel grapes were allowed to become very ripe before picking, and which resulted in wines of approximately 16 degrees of alcohol. The wines were thick, slightly sweet for a red wine, very unusual and, if aged long enough, were wonderful (to some drinker's tastes). They are rarely seen now.

The red
grapes
of Italy

As is true in every major wine producing country, there are hundreds of grape varieties in Italy. Even by the time of Jesus there were dozens of famous Italian wines, according to Pliny, the Roman historian. One of the most famous Italian grape varieties is now known as Zinfandel, and while not much wine is produced from this grape in Italy, it is the basis of the Zinfandel explosion in California.

The two great grapes of Italy today are the NEBBIOLO and the SAN-GIOVESE.

Two others that are becoming more and more popular in the United States are the DOLCETTO and the BARBERA.

Life would be easier if Nebbiolo based wines were called "Nebbiolo," and Sangiovese based wines were called "Sangiovese," but, alas, that is not usually the case.

NEBBIOLO GRAPE BASED WINES:
BAROLO AND BARBARESCO

The Nebbiolo grape is the basis for the greatest wines in Italy. The grape is grown in an area of Northern Italy called the Piedmont, specifically in a part of the Piedmont called the Langhe. The Langhe region of the Piedmont is famous for its hazelnuts, white truffles, good food and good wines. Most of all it's famous for its wines, especially BAROLO.

Unfortunately, far too few people ever have a chance to taste the greatness of the Nebbiolo wines because so few bottles of them are allowed to reach maturity. Barolo in particular usually requires many years in the bottle before it reaches the perfection that has made it great.

The four labels that identify the Nebbiolo wines are BAROLO, BAR-BARESCO, ROERO, and NEBBIOLO (usually followed by "di" and a location; "di" means "from"). Generally of these four types Barolo or Barbaresco wines are likely to appear on most wine lists in the United States. Because of the fame of the names Barolo and Barbaresco, these wines are more often imported into the United States; but I would expect to see more Nebbiolo labels soon because of the escalating prices of the good Barolo and Barbaresco wines.

While there is a great deal of variety in each category, it is traditionally said that the Barolo wines are the more full bodied, and require the most aging, and that the Barbaresco wines are softer in flavor. Nebbiolo is now grown in California, and is sold as a varietal (the word for a wine made from a single type of grape), but the flavors of those that I've tasted so far have little in common with the wines of the Piedmont.

Almost anything you say about Barolo has to be qualified. Traditional Barolo starts life a dark garnet red color with a touch of orange around the rim, and usually lightens with age. Some of the old fashioned techniques cause the coloring material to drop out during aging in barrels, resulting in a lighter wine at the beginning of bottle life. Newer techniques create a wine that is slightly darker in color at this point. The nose is traditionally referred to as a mixture of tar and roses, but what this really refers to is the complexity of tastes in the wine. Typically, at the beginning, there is a deep fruit taste, associated with cherries and plums, followed by the smell of flowers. The nose is often compared to violets and rose petals. Then the power of the wine begins to convey a whole new group of flavors with scents akin to chocolate, coffee, burnt toffee, and anise spice. It is this complexity of flavors and ability to improve with age that makes Barolo the greatest wine produced in Italy.

When young, (during the first five to eight years), Barolo is usually full bodied and tannic, with only a hint of the flavors to come. Many wine drinkers do not appreciate the severe tannic flavor in the young wine made in the traditional style.

In 1991 I drank the last bottle of a case of 1971 Barolo that I bought in the early 1980's. It had turned light red, almost the color of rosé wine. When I poured that last 1971 into a glass, it was like stepping into a rose garden! The room filled with the scent of roses. The taste was of flowers and spice, with little astringency, as the tannins had disappeared with age.

Most Barolo for sale in wine stores today is four to seven years old, deep red, full bodied, strongly grape flavored, with a nose of earth and flowers. There is, of course, a range of quality from different shippers and producers, and from certain vineyards that are sometimes mentioned on the label. But government regulations on production keep the quality reasonably even.

Barolo, and Nebbiolo wines in general, are typically drunk with heavy foods such as meats, stews, wild game and rich sauces which are more often found in cooler climates. In Italy I've seen it used to poach pears, and as a flavoring for risotto. The wine will typically improve if well stored for at least 8-12 years, for Barolo made in the past few years, the better quality wines can age well for 15 to 20 years. You can only predict how well a particular bottle will age by tasting other bottles from the same production every few years. The great years for Barolo were 1971, 1978, 1982, 1985, and 1990.

In Italy during 1995 I could still find a good Barolo or Barbaresco for $8-$10, and good Nebbiolo labeled wines for even less. But the better known wines are at least twice that price, and by the time they appear on the shelves in the United States the price is now more often $20-$35. And, of course, on a restaurant list this increases to $35-$75. This is a lot more than a few years ago, because Barolo and Barbaresco are increasing in fame, while production remains limited.

The best way to acquire a taste for these wines is, naturally, to visit the region, which is just south of Turin, Italy. A lot of literature is given to tourists free of charge, and producers are liberal in giving tastes to visitors.

SANGIOVESE GRAPES:
CHIANTI AND BRUNELLO WINES

The Sangiovese grape forms the basis for a number of wines of varying quality. It is grown all over Italy, but is best known as the major grape in "Chianti" from a particular area of Tuscany, a region in the middle of Italy. Chianti is one of the best-known Italian wines. It is a government-regulated blend (but with latitude in the percentage of various grapes in the mix) of a number of grapes, in which the Sangiovese grape predominates.

Chianti is well known in the U.S. partly because of the pretty straw covered bottles lining the walls of older Italian restaurants. A lot of Chianti was sold because of the distinctive bottles in the 1950's and 60's. Much of that Chianti, along with a lot of Chianti in general, was not very tasty. Some guarantee of quality can be expected from labels that say "Chianti Classico," which means that it was produced in the original Chianti area. But the fact is that many wine makers find it difficult to create a Chianti that is pleasing to today's tastes.

There is somewhat greater variation in Chianti than in Barolo or Barbaresco. This is because there is a central, historical region of Chianti proper (now shown on labels as "Chianti Classico") and a surrounding region that is also entitled to use the name "Chianti." And because Chianti is a blend of various grapes, the percentage of different grapes varies from year to year, creating slightly different flavors. The price range of Chianti can also vary widely, sometimes with no apparent reason.

In the past few years, there has been some success in the attempt to create high quality Chianti to compete in the international market for quality wines. This same push by Italian wine makers has led to an unusual situation for Italian wines. Because of the government's requirement that some amount of white grapes be included in the Chianti blend, certain producers decided to break with the mold and produce a higher quality wine that could not legally use the name "Chianti." They began designating their wines "table wine" instead of the government controlled "Chianti" or "D.O.C.," which means "government controlled name."

As a result of all this, while the words "table wine" are used for wines of lesser quality in most other places in the world, in Italy today those words grace some of the best wine production. This has created a proliferation of labels that makes wines from Tuscany as impossible to identify as those from Burgundy!

In spite of the confusion with labels, one wine which has retained its style and reputation for many generations is the famous Brunello di Montalcino. This wine, made from the Sangiovese grape in one small area of Tuscany, is an excellent representative of the best of the wine that can be made from this grape. Grapes of slightly lower quality harvested in the Montalcino region are used to make "Rosso di Montalcino," a good quality wine which is often sold at very reasonable prices. It is slightly less mellow than Brunello, since it is aged a shorter time in wood. Rosso di Montalcino is also sometimes made from the same grapes as the winemaker's expensive Brunello, when the winemaker runs a bit short of cash and needs to sell some wine without keeping in wood for the length of time required for Brunello. So some rosso's are particularly good buys.

The Sangiovese grape is the hot new item in California at the moment. It is being planted in the hopes of producing a Chianti type wine in California in the next few years. Time will tell.

The flavor and nose of Sangiovese based wines is, to my taste, less complex than in other famous grapes. The wine is medium ruby red in color. The nose is slightly pungent, and more earthy than floral. The Sangiovese grape produces a light-bodied, fruity wine, with a slightly astringent foretaste. It has a crisp, moderately tannic texture, and flavors that remind me of cherries, strawberries, and raspberries mixed together. Sangiovese itself doesn't improve significantly with age and is usually ready to drink when released. But much of the Sangiovese grape is used in blends, like Chianti, which usually age well. Typically it takes between six to 12 years for these blends to reach the peak of maturity. Brunello ages and mellows well with age, four to six years on average, but without as significant a change in color and complexity in taste as the wines made from the Nebbiolo grape.

I would expect to pay between eight to fifteen dollars for a Rosso di Montalcino, and between $25-$75 for a Brunello, depending on the vintage and the producer. The prices for Chianti vary from a few dollars a bottle to $30-40 for special vintages from well-known producers. At the moment 1988, 1989 and 1990 produced the best vintages of the recent years, and the 1997 through 2000 vintages promise well when they are ready to drink.

DOLCETTO AND BARBERA GRAPES

Dolcetto is a wonderful deep purple wine made from the Dolcetto grape grown primarily in the Piedmont region. It doesn't age well, and has a slightly lower alcohol content than wine from the Nebbiolo or the Sangiovese grapes. I believe that is why it "doesn't travel well." That is to say, I've had wonderful Dolcetto in Italy, but the same bottles in Los Angeles have been disappointing. The best known Dolcetto comes from Alba, and has on the label "Dolcetto D'Alba." The wine is ruby-to-violet in color, and has a very distinctive nose that is like nothing else I know. Since the wine does not age well, a recent year on the label —not over one year old— is better than one older than that.

The best-known Barbera wine also comes from Alba, and is labeled "Barbera D'Alba." This is a ruby red wine that darkens slightly as it ages. It starts life very acidic and therefore is sometimes not appreciated when too young. As it ages it loses its acidity and gains in nose and flavor. While it does not age as well as Barolo or Barbaresco, three to six years is generally appropriate. Barbera is a deep, fruity wine reminiscent of raspberries and pomegranate.

Dolcetto and Barbera wines are less well known, and much lower priced than Barolo and Barbaresco. I see these wines selling at wine stores for between six and $15, and in restaurants for roughly twice these amounts, which makes them a good value in today's wine market.

This recipe is from Chef Mark Franz from Farallon in San Francisco. He likes it paired with Ribera del Duero, Janus Tinto Pesquera 1994. Farallon is always on the top 10 in the Zagat Survey. The restaurant is known for its wonderful interior by Pat Kuleto. The light fixtures look like jellyfish floating on the ceiling. The main dining room looks like something out of Captain Nemo's imagination. It's a treat for the eyes, and the food is a treat for the palate:

FARALLON
450 POST STREET
SAN FRANCISCO, CA

KULETO VILLA SQUAB BREAST, MORELS, ENGLISH PEAS AND SPRING ONION SOUBISE

(Makes 4 entrée servings)

INGREDIENTS

4	squab breasts
1/2 bunch	thyme sprigs
2 T	grapeseed, vegetable or olive oil

Spring Onion Soubise:

4 T	*butter*
4 cups	*fresh spring onions, sliced thinly cross-wise*
1/4 cup	*white wine*
	kosher salt and freshly ground pepper
2 cups	*fresh shelled English peas*
3 cups	*fresh morels, cleaned and quartered or 1/2 cup dried*
1/2 bunch	*thyme leaves, finely chopped*
2 T	*olive oil*
2 T	*butter*
	Kosher salt and fresh black pepper
1 T	*grapeseed, vegetable or olive oil*

METHOD

1. To marinate the squab: combine the breasts, oil and thyme for 1 hour to overnight.

2. To make the soubise: in a medium sauté pan over low heat, melt the butter and cook the spring onions until soft, without coloring. When tender, add white wine and reduce over low heat, about 3 minutes. Remove from heat and puree in a blender until very smooth. Season to taste with salt and pepper and keep in a warm place until ready to use.

3. To cook the vegetables: If using dried morels, reconstitute by covering with boiling water. Let sit for one hour. Remove the morels from the liquid and quarter them. Strain and reserve the liquid for another use.

4. In a large sauté pan or skillet, heat the olive oil over medium heat. Add the fresh or reconstituted mushrooms and thyme and cook for 2 to 3 minutes. Add the white wine and English peas and continue to cook until the peas lose their raw taste, about 1 minute. Take off the heat, add the butter, salt and pepper to taste and toss to coat.

5. To cook the squab: Remove the squab from the marinade and season with salt and pepper. Heat olive oil in a medium sauté pan or skillet over high heat for a few seconds. Add the squab, skin-side down and brown, cooking for 3 to 4 minutes each side or to desired doneness. Remove from pan and let rest for up to 5 minutes before cutting into 5 or 6 slices on the bias and serving.

6. To serve, in the middle of each warmed plate, smooth a dollop of the soubise into a circle. Place a scoop of the vegetables on top of the sauce. Fan the slices of squab breast over the vegetables and drizzle a little of the vegetable juices around the plate and over the squab, serve immediately.

Dry White Wine

.

While there are certainly dozens of popular white wine grapes, the market is heavily skewed toward one grape: Chardonnay. Other great white grapes, such as Riesling, Semillon, Sauvignon Blanc and Chenin Blanc are far behind in popularity. The relatively small production of wines made from Rousanne and Marsanne makes these varieties less known. Added to this is the fact that, outside of the U.S., red wine is much more popular than white wine, and by and large more attention is given to its production. Finally, while there are clearly differences in the taste of white grapes, the differences are smaller and more difficult to identify than with red wines.

The result of all this is that you need to know less about white wines than red wines when ordering them from a restaurant list or buying them in a store. Learning the subtleties of flavor of each grape is less important because the method of production determines to the flavor much more than does the grape. Learning a few names to look for on labels, and some geographical references will be helpful.

The questions we hope to answer from looking at labels and price tags on bottles of white wine include: (1) is the wine sweet or dry? (2) is it a tart, acidic wine, or a mellow wine? and (3) is the price reasonable?

Since Semillon and Riesling are the basis for the worlds greatest sweet white wines, let's defer them to the next section on sweet white wines, even though some medium dry white wines are made from these grapes.

That leaves us with the task of learning how to predict the taste of only three white grapes other than the famous Chardonnay: Sauvignon Blanc, Chenin Blanc, and the Rhone wines that usually combine Rousanne and Marsanne (which can be treated together).

CHARDONNAY

This grape is grown all over the world, and more and more vineyards are being cleared of other vines to make room for more of it, because of the strong commercial demand. It is so popular in California that the word is almost synonymous with "white wine," such that one hears waiters ask "would you prefer a glass of red or a glass of Chardonnay?"

Chardonnay is the grape from which Champagne is made, as well as the renowned (and very expensive) white Burgundy wines. Chablis and pouilly Fuissé are made from it. Each of these famous wines has a slightly different taste. Indeed, that is the major characteristic of this grape: it can be molded into a number of wines with different tastes.

I believe that there are basically three different styles of still white wine made from Chardonnay:

First are the mouth-filling, yellow, viscous, oakey, buttery wines. When you look at them they are honey colored. The nose is of ripe fruit and honey. The flavor is oak and pineapple. This used to be a popular style in California but is now somewhat out of vogue. Some of the best Chardonnays in this style come from Australia. This is not a style popular in France, although some wines from Meursault fall into this category.

At the other end of the spectrum are the lean, light colored, fresh, acidic wines more in vogue today. Chablis, from central France, is a good example of this style. It is lightly aromatic, high in acidity, which gives it the ability to age, a slight "flinty-ness" in the best of the Chablis (from the soil), and with an absence of oak, Chablis is a pure form of Chardonnay. Many California producers strive for this style; but the result is usually somewhat different, perhaps because of the lack of chalky soil and the warmer climate.

In the middle of the color spectrum are wines of mild yellow or straw color, medium acidity, a slight fruit nose, and a mild lemon and oak taste. Wines from the Maconnais and Burgundy region are more likely to fall into this category, as are the bulk of those produced on the west coast of the United States. Some of these wines from California have a hint of sweetness not found in the natural grape, which results from the addition of a touch of sugar. (Sugar is also sometimes used in making wine in order to raise alcohol levels).

Some famous names of Chardonnay wines in France are: Pouilly-Fuisse, Montrachet, Macon Blanc, Chablis, Meursault, and Corton-Charlemagne. Of course, in the United States and in Australia (and now sometimes in Italy) the label will contain the word "Chardonnay."

Chardonnay is not generally aged, and is usually drunk soon after bottling. I've found, however, that those aged in oak will improve in flavor after two or three years in the bottle.

There is a wide range of prices for Chardonnay, with prices in California for the well known labels somewhat higher than for the same quality in a French or Australian Chardonnay. At the low end you can find a reasonable Chardonnay for four dollars a bottle, but the bulk of the market is in the eight to $15 range. Some high end producers in California, and well known French Chablis may run as high as $50, and the great Burgundies, such as Montrachet, in good years sell in the $50-$150 range.

Thus, there is no one easily distinguishable "Chardonnay taste," and it can only be identified by knowing the label, or perhaps by a process of elimination. In spite of its great financial success, there is the beginning of a tendency today away from Chardonnay in some quarters, toward other white grapes with more distinctive characteristics.

Nancy Oakes of Boulevard Restaurant in San Francisco, which is the #1 favorite in the Zagat Guide for San Francisco, favors Poached Turbot and Morel Mushrooms with Domenique La Font Chassagne Montrachet wine. Although her husband, Bruce Aidells, "The Sausage King", author of ten cookbooks, likes to pair Pomard from the Burgundy area of France with a Crispy Duck with Sour Cherries. He has sent us a recipe for Moroccan Cous-Cous with Fruit and Pistachios.

POACHED TURBOT
AND MOREL MUSHROOMS
(Serves 2)

Recipe by Judy Lamm

INGREDIENTS

3	*morel mushrooms*
1 tsp	*butter*

64

1	*shallot, minced*
1/3 cup	*dry white wine or white Vermouth*
1/4 tsp	*fish or chicken base*
pinch	*tarragon*
pinch	*thyme*
1/3 cup	*cream*
12 oz.	*fillet of turbot*
	fresh lemon juice
	fresh ground pepper

METHOD

1. Soak morels in water to dislodge dirt. Remove and rinse well. Slice.

2. Heat butter in a sauté pan, and sauté shallots until translucent. Deglaze the pan with 1/3 cup wine, leaving about 2 T of liquid. Add 1/4 tsp fish or chicken base, pinch of tarragon and pinch of ground thyme (or a branch of fresh) and 1/3 cup cream and mix while on low heat. Stir in mushrooms. (Remove branch of thyme, if using.)

3. Sprinkle turbot with a little lemon juice and freshly ground pepper.

4. Turn up heat to medium and place fillets on top of cream mixture. Cover, and poach for about 2 to 3 minutes per side, or until fish just flakes, but is moist inside.

TO DO IN A.M.: Steps 1 and 2

TO DO A DAY IN ADVANCE: Step 1

TO FREEZE: If you have any left over, you can freeze and reheat in microwave, but it won't be quite as good.

BRUCE AIDELLS'
MOROCCAN COUSCOUS
WITH FRUIT AND PISTACHIOS

Serves 6

2	cups chicken stock
3	tbsp olive oil
1/4	lb Moroccan sausage, diced
1	small onion, diced
1 1/3	cups couscous
1/4	cup chopped dried apricots
1/4	cup golden raisins
6	Aidells Moroccan Sausage with Pistachios
1/4	cup shelled pistachios
1	tbsp chopped, fresh mint
	Salt and freshly ground black pepper

Preheat the oven to 350°. Bring the stock to a boil in a saucepan. Heat 1 tbsp of the olive oil in a skillet over medium heat, stir in onion and sausage, and cook 4-5 minutes, browning slightly. Add the couscous, apricots and raisins and stir until well coated. Pour in the boiling chicken stock, remove from heat, cover and let stand for about 15 minutes. In a heavy skillet over medium heat fry the whole sausages for 2-3 minutes a side until well browned, set aside.

Stir the remaining ingredients into the couscous and mix well. Season to taste with salt and pepper. Spoon the couscous onto a serving platter and arrange the browned sausages on top, serve.

SAUVIGNON BLANC
(also known as Fumé Blanc)

Wine from this grape, at least in the United States, is on the upswing as an alternative to Chardonnay. The wine is dry, slightly tart and mouth cleansing, with a nose often referred to as that of unripe fruit (as opposed to the more lush nose of the Chardonnay, which is more like ripe fruit). The current popularity of these wines arises from their refreshing, zesty taste that goes well with foods that are not rich or fatty. When not well made, however, the result is a wine with little or no aroma or taste, and sometimes excessive acidity. The well-made wines are known for their tart taste and strong aromatic nose.

One of the best-known labels is Sancerre, from the Loire Valley in France. Another well-known label is Pouilly-Fumé, from the same area. In California wines from this grape are labeled Sauvignon Blanc, or Fumé Blanc.

Good Sancerre is particularly prized for a slight flinty taste that arises from the chalky soil in which it is grown.

These wines do not improve with age. But when added to the juice of other grapes, as is done in various areas of France, the combination sometimes produces wines of longer life.

A lot of cheap Sauvignon is produced that lacks the essential character of the grape. And because the name still lacks the popularity of Chardonnay, a good bottle is still relatively inexpensive—in the range of six to $12. A few producers both in California and in France have developed a reputation for fine Sauvignon Blanc (or Pouilly Fumé), and these wines sell in the $12-$35 range.

Seiji Wakabayashi is an inspired chef, formerly of Ondine Restaurant in Sausalito, and currently of Pascal in Newport Beach, California. His culinary expertise turns out the most delicious food. For us, he has chosen Meret Soliel Tieana Blanc, 1997, to be paired with:

LOBSTER SALAD WITH CHRYSANTHEMUM LEAVES AND SWEET GINGER CREAM

INGREDIENTS

1	*live Maine lobster (about 11/2 lbs)*
1 cup	*white wine*
1/4 cup	*onion (chopped)*
1/4 cup	*celery (chopped)*
2 quarts	*water*
	salt and freshly ground pepper to taste

Sweet Ginger Cream:

1 cup	*good quality mayonnaise*
2 T	*pickled ginger (chopped)*
	pickled ginger juice to taste

Salad:

2 cups	*chrysanthemum leaves*
	(available in Japanese markets or substitute baby greens)
2 T	*yellow papaya (diced)*
2 T	*crisp bacon (diced)*
2 T	*green papaya (diced)*
1 oz	*curry oil*

68

METHOD

In large saucepan, prepare a court bouillon, by combining the white wine, chopped onion, carrot and celery. Add water and season with salt and pepper. Bring mixture to a boil over medium-high heat. Reduce heat and simmer 10 minutes. Add the lobster and poach for 5 to 8 minutes. Remove lobster to a work surface. When cool, slice lobster in half lengthwise. Remove meat from tail and claws. Reserve tail half shells. Slice tail meat and put back into shells. Top with claw meat. Make sweet ginger cream in a bowl by combining the mayonnaise, pickled ginger and pickled ginger juice. Mix well and set aside.

PRESENTATION

Place the chrysanthemum leaves, bacon and green papaya in a salad bowl. Spoon ginger cream over the mixture (be sure to reserve some of the ginger cream for lobster meat) and toss. Divide the greens between 2 salad plates. Place lobster halves in the center of the greens. Drizzle lobster with remaining ginger cream. Garnish with diced yellow papaya and a drizzle with curry oil.

There are a lot of dry, crisp white wines from little known grapes. Here is an example of such a chef's favorite wine coupled with a recipe:

This recipe for Roasted Garlic Profiteroles, which Brian Weselby, corporate chef for the Napa Valley Grilles located throughout the U.S., likes to pair with 1998 Enotria Arneis, Mendocino. The restaurants feature "Perfect Pairs," which are small bites designed to blend with carefully chosen premium wines. Some of the Perfect Pairs might be Seared Diver Scallop, foie gras-quince vinaigrette, paired with 1999 Robert Mondavi Pinot Grigio, Napa; or Crisp Rock Shrimp Ravioli, green tomato lemon salad, chile sauce, paired with 1999 Firestone Gewurztraminer, Santa Barbara; or Thyme Crusted Ahi Tuna, grilled pineapple and pineapple foam paired with 1997 Camelot Pinot Noir, California.

Brian's background includes association with two Michelin-starred restaurants — Chewton Glen Hotel in Bournemouth, England, and the Hotel Metropole, Beaulieu Sur Mer, France.

ROASTED GARLIC PROFITEROLES

Olive Salad, White Truffle Cheese

INGREDIENTS

1 cup	water
3 1/2 oz	butter
1 T	Kosher salt
pinch	sugar
5	eggs
6 1/2 fl oz	measured flour
1 T	thyme and rosemary, mixed
6 fl oz	measured Parmesan cheese, grated fine
	salt and pepper to taste

To make the profiteroles:

Boil water, butter and salt with sugar. Add in flour and herbs all at once. Cook until it pulls from the sides. Beat in eggs one at a time. Add in cheese and herbs.

Scoop dough into piping bag. Pipe out marble-sized balls onto a greased cookie sheet. Bake at 350 degrees for 18-20 minutes, until golden brown. Leave to cool.

To make the garlic cream stuffing:

1/2 cup	*garlic cloves, peeled*
1/4 cup	*olive oil*
1/4 cup	*water*

Combine all ingredients and cook slowly over low heat until the garlic is very soft. Puree in a Cuisinart. Pipe a small amount into cooled profiteroles.

Olive Salad:

1 cup	*each olives (3 varieties)*

Slice olives. Drizzle with extra virgin olive oil, a sprinkle of chopped thyme, salt and pepper.

To assemble:

1 T	*olive salad*
2	*filled profiteroles*
	shaved truffle cheese or Parmesan cheese
	sprinkle with chopped chives and cracked black pepper

Medium Dry Wines

(SLIGHTLY SWEET)

CHENIN BLANC

This grape generally produces a less dry wine with at least a definite hint of sweetness. You won't see much of this wine around. Limited amounts are grown in the Loire Valley in France, and much of it is used in blends. In California it is sometimes used to make a sweet, inexpensive wine. One of the most common labels seen in the United States indicates production from "Vouvray," a region in France where the Chenin Blanc grape is used to make four kinds of wine: dry, medium, sweet, and sparkling Vouvray (frequently seen in the United States). This grape is particularly important in South African wine production, which is growing in popularity in the United States. The Chenin Blanc grape is now sometimes seen in the United States as Anjou Blanc, a popular production from the Loire Valley in France. Rosé d'Anjou, with a similar taste, used to be very popular in the 1950's and 1960's in the United States, before the craze for dry white wine.

The wine is light straw in color, with a light floral aroma. Its main characteristic is very high acidity, particularly when the wine is young. Because of the high acidity, the wine ages well and improves with age, for as long as 20 years. Sometimes this wine, even when produced as a still wine, will have a slight tingle like very small bubbles, which makes it particularly refreshing.

Because of the range of styles, when buying or ordering a wine from the Chenin Blanc grape it is important to look at the label for clues, or to ask, if you are to know if you will be drinking a dry, medium, or sweet wine, and whether or not it is still or sparkling.

The wines from this grape are among the least expensive wines of those discussed in this book, and can be found at prices between eight to $20. These wines are now attracting more and more interest, again, as an alternative to the more expensive Chardonnay.

ROUSSANNE & MARSANNE

These two grapes, in varying percentages, are responsible for the white wines of the Rhone Valley in France. While still little known, they produce a wine that has, for many people, just the right proportion of dryness to sweetness, a wonderful floral nose, and the ability to age well. As a result of these favorable characteristics these wines are becoming more and more popular, the grapes are being planted in more and more vineyards, and several of the most famous vineyards are putting their names on labels with these wines representing their production of white wine.

There is no outstanding distinguishing feature about the flavor of these grapes, and the taste characteristics vary greatly depending on the mix of grapes and the style of production. The two main attributes that characterize this group of wines are (1) they are not dry, crisp, pale wines; rather they are medium bodied, straw or honey colored with a fairly strong grape taste and medium high acidity; and (2) there is a particular light and pleasing floral nose that, for some, makes food taste better. The Marsanne grape gives smooth body and viscosity to the wine, and the Rousanne grape gives the floral nose and the aging potential.

Some of the famous Chateaux in the Rhone region of France that are producing wines from these grapes, and their labels, are: Hermitage Blanc, Paul Jaboulet Ainè, St. Peray (often sparkling), Chateauneuf-du-Pape Blanc, and Chateau de Beaucastel Blanc. By and large, any wine labeled Cote du Rhone Blanc is likely to be made from these grapes.

Lack of demand would ordinarily keep down the prices of these wines, but the small production has kept them up. Those wines produced by the famous red wine producers are fairly expensive, perhaps $15-$35; but those wines produced by less well known producers have remained in the eight to $15 range, which makes them an excellent buy for wines of such good quality and ability to enhance the pleasure of dining.

Sweet White Wines

This is a wonderful subject about some wondrous wines. But sweet wines are pretty easy to identify after you've tasted them once, and you need very little information to enjoy them. Yes, there is a lot you can learn, for example, about different types of Ports and Sherrys. But that is beyond the scope of this book, which is about basics.

Dry and sweet Ports and Sherrys have a distinctive taste that you can instantly identify just by drinking a glass at a bar. But there are two specific flavors of sweet wines that you should know about, along with some information about the labels that go with them, because they appear so often on wine lists.

RIESLING

This is one of the most famous grapes in the world—(some say that German Riesling is the greatest wine made), with a special taste that—once tasted— you will not forget; but not much of it is consumed in the United States. Like mango and Lychee nuts, it just isn't a taste that has become popular. Because of the shifting market toward dry white wines, some of the traditional production of sweet Riesling in both Germany (the home of the great Rieslings) and California has been shifted toward "dry Riesling," which I would describe as a medium dry, or slightly sweet, wine. But the great Rieslings are those produced for centuries on the steep slopes of the Rhine valley in Germany, and these bottles, (with labels containing long 20-letter German words to identify the characteristics of the wine), are wines that become something special after years of aging in the bottle. This is another vine that Pliny wrote about in the First Century, and some of the current wine makers trace their ancestry back to the 15th century.

These wines have little in common with the medium dry California Rieslings, the more recent (and popular) late harvest California Rieslings, or even the well loved Rieslings of Alsace, a region of France near Germany. Each of these wines also has its following, but they are not the same as the great Rieslings of Germany, produced by this group of old-time, famous producers. There are also a few wines labeled as Riesling, particularly from South American countries, that are not made from Riesling grapes at all.

The essential characteristics of the fine wines from this grape are a tart, strongly aromatic wine (like Sauvignon Blanc) with an exceptional impact on the nose, as well as the taste buds, and a long-lasting after-taste. The taste is as distinct as an exotic fruit, and reminds me of ripe, exotic tropical fruits, marinated in honey. The wine begins life as a green-gold liquid, and darkens slightly with age. The taste remains fresh, with fairly high acidity, while the alcohol level is often very low—sometimes containing half as much as other wines.

These great wines are in strong demand, and the production is limited. In fact, great Rieslings are not produced every year because of climatic conditions. A bottle bearing a coveted designation, such as Trockenbeerenauslesen, is likely to cost upwards of $100, and that is before you bear the cost of aging it for 15 or 20 years. But for about $30-$50 you can find some of the very good Rieslings, and they can be enjoyed after a few years in the bottle.

James Chew, former Chef at Stars in San Francisco and Vong in New York, favors a pairing of Bonny Doon Pacific Rim Reisling with a recipe for Pad Thai with Garnishes:

PAD THAI WITH GARNISHES
(4 servings)

INGREDIENTS
1 pound dried pad Thai rice noodles-soaked in water for 30 minutes, drained

Sauce:
1/4 cup	*tamarind water-see TECHNIQUE instructions*
1/4 cup	*tomato paste*
3/4 cup	*water*
1 1/2 T	*sugar*
3 T	*Thai fish sauce*
1/4 tsp	*white pepper*

Cooked Garnishes:
1 tsp	*garlic-minced*
3 pieces	*shallots-thinly sliced*
1/2 cup	*onions-1" long slices*
2 T	*diced preserved radishes*
1/4 cup	*aged tofu-cut into 1/2" long x 1/4" wide pieces*
1 T	*Asian dried shrimp-soaked in water for 30 minutes*

| 8 ounces | shrimp-small, shelled, deveined |
| 4 T | canola oil |

Fresh Garnishes:

3/4 cup	fresh bean sprouts
8 pieces	lime wedges
1/4 cup	peanuts-roasted, unsalted, coarse chopped
1 T	chili flakes
1/2 cup	scallions-green and white parts, 1" long julienne
1/2 cup	coriander sprigs

EQUIPMENT/SUPPLIES

Small sauce pot; wok or large fry pan and utensils; kitchen tongs; strainer; spatula.

TECHNIQUE

1) Make tamarind water. Take 2" square piece of tamarind pulp and combine with 3/4 cup warm water in bowl. Mash pulp into water and mix until pulp dissolves. Press through strainer with spatula and reserve.

2) Make sauce. Bring all sauce ingredients to simmer in sauce pot and cook 5 minutes. Cool and reserve.

3) Cook garnishes and noodles. Heat oil in wok over high heat. Add and stir fry ingredients in following order: garlic, shallots, onions, dried shrimps, radish, tofu-cook several minutes until onions soft; shrimp-season all ingredients lightly with salt and pepper and stir fry until shrimp just turns red but still tender; pad Thai noodles, sauce-stir fry several more minutes until noodles are soft. Adjust seasoning and arrange in center of warm platter.

4) Arrange fresh garnishes on platter. Place piles of fresh garnishes around edges of platter surrounding noodles. Serve family style. Each guest takes a portion of noodles and whatever garnishes desired mixing together with noodles, and always squeezes lime juice on the top of garnished noodles.

SEMILLON

Finally we come to the other extremely highly prized sweet wine of the western world. These wines are named Sauternes after the area of France where the greatest examples are produced. And like Riesling, while many admire its taste and greatness, few buy it and drink it. The Semillon grape, from which Sauternes is made, is used primarily for blending with other grapes, to give them more body and fullness. Not much is grown in California. It is important in Australia and Chile in the production of various blends of white wines.

It is really only in France that this grape is grown in quantities sufficient to constitute a significant percentage of total grape production, and this is true primarily in the Bordeaux and neighboring regions. White Bordeaux, from various Chateaux, usually contains some percentage of this grape. Typical labels of wine from this grape that are seen on U.S. wine lists include: Cotes de Bordeaux, Côtes de Blaye, and Côtes de Bergerac. These wines are typically medium dry, slightly oily full-bodied white wines, which are not noted for any particular taste or nose. They are low in acidity, and thus do not age well, but when aged in oak, as they typically are, they take on a mellow oakey flavor.

But in the Sauternes region, these thin skinned grapes are allowed to develop the famous "noble rot" that, in some years, produces a rich, pale yellow liquid that explodes with sweetness on the tongue, and lingers there for some time. As it ages, it darkens slightly and develops a slight reddish, or red-brown color component. The taste changes from honey and fruit to a more complex, fruit, butterscotch, slightly less sweet, and sometimes slightly burnt flavor unique to this grape. While much of the production is drunk during the first five years after bottling, to achieve this special flavor aging between ten to twenty years is common.

Far and away the most famous producer of this kind of wine is Chateau d'Yquem in the Sauternes area of France. Wines from this Chateau are collected each year (that the wine is produced, which is not every year) by thousands of collectors. As a result, the price of these wines is beyond the point of interest to most wine drinkers. Bottles from the lesser years are now at $100 or more, and from the good years often $200 and up. The small, half-sized bottles are quite popular and can be found in many wine stores, but not in much quantity.

Another Chateau in Sauternes that is well known, but whose wine is much less expensive is Chateau Rieussec; a number of other chateaux in the Sauternes region produce a slightly lesser example of this wine. Adjacent to the Sauternes region is Barsac, with very similar, but slightly less sweet wines.

So when you see Sauternes or Barsac on a wine list, expect it to be very sweet. This does not necessarily mean that it is a dessert wine (although it is frequently listed that way on wine lists). Many wine drinkers like a sweet wine with a fruit course, or with some very rich dishes, such as goose liver pâté.

Rosé, Sparkling and other Wines

There are so many grapes and wines that I haven't mentioned. There are the wonderful wines made from the Trebbiano grapes of Italy. Everyone knows something about Champagne. In many areas of Europe sparkling wines, including sparkling red wines (such as Lambrusco in the Veneto region of Northern Italy) are preferred by most of the local wine drinking population. There are hundreds of wonderful local red wines throughout Europe. But they're not on U.S. wine lists very often, and what I've written about is enough to learn for a beginning—except for the Rosé wines. It's nice to know something about them.

Rosé wine is made from red grapes. The grape skins, which give red wine its color and tannin, are not left in contact with the juice for very long, so the juice doesn't become as red as it otherwise would. This makes the wine rose colored, less tannic, and more delicate in flavor—-all depending on the winemaker's decision on how long to leave the skins in contact with the juice. Because of the range of decision that the winemaker has, some consider rosé wine to have a wider range of flavors than red or white wines.

The southern French have a saying that goes: a wine drinker begins by enjoying white wine, matures into preferring red wine, and ends up loving rosé.

There is some truth to that in the south of France. Located in a hot part of a country that loves red wine, chilled rosé is a good substitute during hot weather, and has become very popular. But, by and large, that hasn't become the case in the United States, although in the 1950's sparkling rosé from Portugal became a fad, and the medium sweet Rosé d'Anjou was moderately popular.

Today there is only one rosé that is on virtually every California wine list: white Zinfandel, a medium sweet, full-bodied, rich rose-colored wine. The huge financial success of this wine is at odds with the trend toward lighter Chardonnay. It may indicate that there are a number of wine drinkers who don't care for light, acidic white wines and would appreciate some of the less dry, full bodied white wines I've mentioned before, if they knew about them and could identify them on a wine list.

Perhaps rosé other than white Zinfandel will make a comeback soon. That would be good news for many wine drinkers because there are interesting rosé wines of almost every character. Those most popular in the south of France, such as Chateau Minuty, are very dry, and hard to distinguish from white wines except for a slightly stronger flavor. The rosé wines of Anjou and the Loire valley tend to be slightly sweet, with a floral nose and flavor. Many of the California rosé wines are fairly sweet.

But in France and Italy rosé is made from many of the leading red grapes. I recently had a delightful rosé in the hills of San Damiano, in northern Italy, made from Pinot Noir grapes. The wine retained some of the characteristic flavor of the Pinot Noir grape, but was more delicate than a red Pinot Noir.

At the moment rosé (other than white Zinfandel) is not featured on many wine lists, but it is something worth trying. Unless you recognize the label, however, such as one of those mentioned above, it may be difficult, without asking, to predict whether the wine you order will be sweet or dry, and what the taste will be like.

Serving Wine: Customs and Traditions

WINE WITH FOOD

While many folks drink a glass of wine for an aperitif, most wine is consumed with food. Some people have relatively fixed ideas about which wines go with which foods, such as white wines with fish, Bordeaux with lamb, and rosé only at a summer picnic; but I'm not one of those people. Still, there are certain basic ideas that most wine drinkers hold about matching wines and foods, and some of these ideas are expressed below. In addition, I love to cook with wine, and I've included a few of my favorite recipes below as examples of how wine can enhance cooking.

MILD (DELICATE) FLAVORS

Certain foods have a delicate taste that can disappear if the taste of the wine is too strong. This is true of some fish, depending on how it is cooked, and many raw foods. With these foods I prefer a dry wine that also has a delicate, mild flavor, often with an elevated acidity level.

For example, with oysters I like a mild, light, flinty, acidic dry white wine. Those Chablis wines, with a dry "chalky" flavor, are particularly good with oysters, and with poached or pan-fried white fish. Scallops and abalone are other examples of delicate tastes. These mild seafood flavors seem to me to go best with mild, acidic white wines. Popular wines for these dishes are the California Sauvignon Blanc's, and the Muscadet and Sancerre wines of the Loire valley in France. There is little doubt in my mind that most fish in California, if not the entire United States, is eaten with a glass of Chardonnay, but I personally find many Chardonnays to be too flavorful with oak and rich, buttery fruit taste to go well with these delicate tastes. As they say in French: chaque'un a son gout.

STRONG TASTES

Not all fish are mild in flavor. Salmon, for example, has a strong, distinctive flavor. Monkfish often has a strong flavor, and some smoked fish have a very strong, lingering flavor. Most marinated herrings have strong flavors of dill, onion, or other marinades. Cioppino, cooked in a tomato, garlic and oregano based broth, is also not delicate in flavor. With salmon and cioppino I prefer rosé wines, or a light red, such as Beaujolais. Many wine lovers prefer a strong flavored white wine, such as a German Riesling, with such dishes.

The inverse is also true: not all meats have a strong flavor. Many consider veal to be a delicate flavor that can be overwhelmed by a strong red wine. For this reason many prefer a mild white wine, or a very light red wine with veal dishes. Of course, this depends in part on how the veal is cooked, and what sauce is served with it.

There are, of course, a lot of diverse strong flavors. Spicy food is one category. Personally, I prefer beer with spicy foods, but a fruity Côte du Rhone, or not-too-dry rosé is also good.

Then of course there are the strong flavors of certain meats; barbecue and wild game are examples. The full bodied red wines are usually preferred for these flavors, such as Barolo, Hermitage, Zinfandel and Côte du Rhone's. Good Bordeaux and Burgundies, of course, can go well with such flavors, but traditionally the top notch wines are usually reserved for foods that will not detract too much from the flavors of the wines; in other words, a really good Bordeaux or Burgundy should be the star flavor of the course, not an assistant. A good Bordeaux, for me, goes particularly well with a plain, simply cooked steak. The explosive taste of a fine Burgundy, for me, calls for light, simple foods that do not interfere with the taste of the wine.

TRADITIONAL PAIRINGS

Since food and wine are strongly influenced by culture, there are, naturally, certain food and wine combinations that are often thought of together, whether it makes sense or not.

The French like rich goose liver (foie gras) with sweet Sauternes, particularly in December. I can remember having this combination at a wine bar across from the Church of the Madeleine in Paris, and thinking I was in heaven!

In many fine restaurants, Bordeaux is recommended with lamb dishes. Personally I prefer Burgundy with lamb, and Bordeaux with beef.

In the Piedmont, Barolo is served with wild game and rich, fatty red meats.

Chicken dishes are often served with Beaujolais or a light Burgundy, depending on the sauce. The custom is to serve darker wines with tomato based sauces, light red wines with natural sauces, and fruity white wines with sauces based on white wine or Champagne.

These traditional combinations are worth knowing about, and often following, but the trend in cooking during the past decade has been more experimental, and much less rigid. Salmon is often served now in red wine sauce, and white wine, with various herbs is frequently used as the base, along with stock, for meat sauces. The recent trend toward drinking red wine, for health reasons, has led toward an attitude of "red wine with anything."

With such combinations now in vogue, most of the traditional rules no longer apply, except the basic rule with which we started the chapter:

Foods that have a delicate taste require delicate wines so that the taste of the food is not obscured; strong flavored foods need full bodied wines that can stand up to the flavor of the food.

Here are a few recipes that use wine (in different ways) and are very easy and quick to make, from Merv and Judy's favorite ways to use up leftover wines:

Recipes

Merv's Favorite Recipes

CABBAGE & BONES IN BAROLO

Ingredients:

1	white onion, grated
1 T.	olive oil
3 pieces	bacon, optional)
1 to 3 lbs.	Ribs (pork, lamb or beef)
2 to 4 pieces	of chicken or duck, optional)
1	red cabbage, cut into small pieces
	sage or tarragon to taste
	salt & pepper to taste
1/3 bottle	(1 liter) of Barolo wine
1 tsp.	Balsamic vinegar
	pinch sugar

METHOD

1. Grate a white onion into a large pan with a good cover and place it on top of the stove. (I use a pan 14 inches in diameter and about 2 inches high.) Saute' the onion in a small amount of olive oil with or without a few pieces of bacon. Rain out the fat/oil, and add some ribs. Adding cut-up chicken or duck is good, but optional. Or you can use a mixture of these meats. If you're using this as a main course with meat, but in enough meat to serve four to six people. Brown meat to cook off the fat.

2. Meanwhile, dice up a whole purple cabbage into small pieces. When the meat is browned, add the cabbage (or as much as your pot will take). Add some seasoning, depending on the kind of meat you used and your taste. I like lamb or pork ribs and then add sage, with chicken I use tarragon. If you like salt, sprinkle some into the pot, Then pour about a third of a bottle of the Barolo you're drinking with dinner into the pot; it should be enough wine to wet the cabbage and leave about 1/4 inch in the bottom of the pot. Add 1 tsp. of aged balsamic vinegar and a pinch of sugar. Stir the seasonings around, cover the pot loosely, leaving a small opening on one side, and let it cook on a low fire for about an hour, until the wine is fully absorbed into the cabbage, and the cabbage has changed texture and darkened in color. Open another bottle of Barolo as a backup, and serve to four to six people. If you're too cheap to serve Barolo, use Barbera.

TO PREPARE IN A.M.: Steps 1 & 2

TO PREPARE A DAY IN ADVANCE: Steps 1& 2

TO FREEZE: Steps 1 & 2

CHICKEN IN CHAMPAGNE SAUCE

(Note: White wine is often mixed with butter and cream to create a rich sauce.)

INGREDIENTS:

1	*onion*
1 T.	*butter*
1 T.	*olive oil*
2	*garlic cloves, minced*
6 - 8 pieces	*frying chicken*
5 oz.	*(1/2 can) chicken broth*
5 oz.	*champagne or medium dry white wine*
	cream

METHOD:

1. Brown an onion in butter and olive with minced garlic in a wide stove-top pan, and then add pieces of chicken and brown them until the fat is off the skin and the skin is brown. Add 5 oz. chicken broth (if its not the salt free kind, it will contain enough salt for this dish) and an equal amount of champagne or wine (I find champagne works best here) depending on your taste preference for salty or sweet foods. Put a cover on loosely, so steam can get out, and stew the chicken over a low flame for 30-40 minutes until it is cooked through. Take the chicken out of the pan, and put it into a covered pot to keep it warm. Then turn up the fire and reduce the wine sauce by 1/3 or so. When it's reduced, turn the fire down to low, add an amount of cream approximately rqual to 1/2 the amount of liquid left after the reduction. Stir the sauce, and put the chicken back in to warm up. Serve the chicken with rice or noodles and spoon some sauce over both the chicken and the rice (or noodles).

TO PREPARE IN A.M.: Step 1

TO PREPARE A DAY IN ADVANCE: Step 1

TO FREEZE: Step 1

SAUTEED DUCK BREAST
THROUGH ROSE COLORED GLASSES

(Note: With fowl an game birds re or rose' wine is often combined with a stewed fruit or fruit jam/jelly as an agent to add fruit flavor and thickening. This dish is easier to make if you buy only the breast, either whole or sliced. But, if you're a purist you can buy a fresh or frozen duck (or goose), thaw out the frozen bird overnight, and roast or grill the duck for 30 minutes either on a hot grill, or in the oven at 375'F). Then slice several pieces from the breast and thighs. You may prefer to use a cut up duck. The important thing is to get some of the fat out before the saute'ing process begins. If you start with a boned breast, cook it through on the grill or in the oven (about 10 minutes) to make it easier to slice, then slice it into thin slices. Sprinkle a pinch of salt over it if you like.)

INGEDIENTS:

1	duck breast
2 T.	olive oil
1 C.	dry or medium rose' wine
1 T.	seedless raspberry jam
	salt to taste

METHOD:

1. Saute' the duck slices in olive oil 5 minutes or so until cooked through, then take the out and put on a covered plate. Add a cup of a dry or medium rose', such as a Rose D'Anjou or one of the many roses from the Cote du Rhone, and boil the hell out of it until it's reduced by 1/2. Then add a spoonful of seedless raspberry jam (or some other dark berry), and stir it into the sauce. Keep reducing the sauce until it begins to thicken, then put the slices back in to warm them up for a minute and serve. I like it over wild rice.

STEAK IN RED WINE SAUCE

(Note: This traditional recipe illustrates the use of wine reduction sauce in a skillet-based dish.)

INGREDIENTS:

1	onion, sliced
1	clove garlic, crushed
1 oz.	butter
1 tsp.	olive oil
	pinch salt
6 oz.	filet mignon (or larger)
1 slice	toast, crusts removed
	(1 slice foie gras, optional)
1/4 C.	full bodied red wine
1/4 C.	beef bouillon
1	mushroom cap, sautéed, or one slice truffle, optional

METHOD:

1. Sauté one sliced onion and one crushed garlic clove in 1 oz. of butter, 1 tsp. olive oil and a pinch of salt. Brown one filet per person in the butter and onion, until almost done to your taste. Take out the steak and put it on a slice of toast. Some people add a slice of foie gras on top of the toast. Pour about 1/4 C. of a full bodied red wine and 1/4 C. of beef bouillon into the skillet, turn up the fire and cook the hell out of it until it is reduced down to about 3 T. of sauce per filet (this will take some time, and the sauce will thicken quite a bit). Spoon the sauce over the filets, add a mushroom cap or piece of black truffle on top, and serve with a full bodied red wine and a sharp knife to anyone with cholesterol under 200.

HAROSET

This middle-eastern dish makes a wonderful appetizer on a hot summer night, and is a typical use of wine as a fruit marinade.

INGREDIENTS:

1	*apple*
	lemon juice
1 T.	*raisins*
1 T.	*chopped almonds*
1 T.	*chopped dates*
	Sweet wine

METHOD:

1. Peel and cut into small bite-sized pieces, one apple per serving, pouring lemon juice over the apples before and after cutting, to preserve their color. (Golden Delicious apples don't discolor as quickly as others.) For each serving add 1 T. each of raisins, chopped almonds and dates. Soak in a sweet wine (any color you prefer), stir well, drain any excess wine, and serve chilled. (If you have a leftover bottle of wine you prefer to use that is not a sweet wine, you can use it and add sugar).

Judy's Favorites

The following recipes are those which Judy serves especially with the wines indicated.

Dry Sherry or Champagne

These make a wonderful appetizer
or they can be served with steak:

MUSHROOMS BRAISED IN OYSTER SAUCE

INGREDIENTS

1 lb	*fresh button mushrooms*
5 T	*butter*
2 tsp	*oyster sauce*
2 T	*dry Sherry*
1 tsp	*sugar*
2 tsp	*soy sauce*
	seasoned salt to taste - optional

METHOD

1. Clean mushrooms and dry - leave whole.
2. Melt butter and sauté mushrooms slowly until golden. Add oyster sauce, 2 T Sherry, 1 tsp sugar, 2 tsp soy sauce and seasonings to taste.
3. Cook and stir until nearly dry. Serve hot.

TO PREPARE IN MORNING: Steps 1 and 2

TO PREPARE DAY BEFORE: Steps 1 and 2

TO FREEZE: May make steps 1 through 3 and reheat; be careful not to make sauce too dry, because you'll need liquid to reheat.

This recipe is really delicious. Use as an appetizer or vegetable side dish:

TURKISH ZUCCHINI ROUNDS (MÜCVER)
(Serves 10 to 12)

INGREDIENTS

5 cups	grated zucchini (6 small or 4 medium)
3	eggs (extra large), beaten
6	green onions, whole, minced
2 T	chopped dill weed
1/2 cup	chopped fresh mint
1/2 cup	chopped fresh parsley
1 cup	grated Swiss cheese
11/2 cups	flour
	salt, pepper - to taste
1/8 tsp	cayenne
	oil for frying (peanut preferred)

METHOD

1. Put the grated zucchini into a large bowl and add the beaten eggs, minced green onions, 2 T dill, 1/2 cup chopped mint, 1/2 cup chopped parsley, 1 cup grated cheese. Add the flour a small amount at a time, mixing well. Add the salt, pepper and cayenne.

2. In a frying pan, heat the oil to 350 to 400 degrees. You should have a thin layer of oil about 1/8" to 1/4" deep. Drop the zucchini mixture by tablespoonfuls, one at a time, into the oil, being careful not to crowd the pan. When golden brown on one side, turn and fry other side till golden brown.

3. Serve hot as a vegetable with dinner, or smaller rounds may be made using teaspoonfuls and served as hot hors d'oeuvres.

TO PREPARE IN A.M.: Steps 1 and 2, reheat on rack in oven.

TO PREPARE A DAY IN ADVANCE: Steps 1 and 2, reheat on rack in oven.

TO FREEZE: Steps 1 and 2, reheat on rack in oven.

Save your money on commercial lox and make this easy and much better tasting gravad lax:

GRAVAD LAX - (SCANDINAVIAN)

INGREDIENTS

4-lb piece	salmon or filet
2/3 cup	coarse salt (Kosher salt)
1 T	fresh ground black pepper
1/2 C	sugar
1 T	Cognac
1-2 bunches	fresh dill

METHOD

1. Split the salmon and remove the bones

2. Mix together 2/3 C coarse salt, 1 T freshly ground black pepper, 1/2 cup sugar. Sprinkle 1 T Cognac over the flesh. Rub the salt mixture into the flesh of the salmon.

3. Line a deep bowl or dish well with sprigs of fresh dill. Lay one half the salmon over the dill, skin side down. Arrange a thick layer of dill sprigs over the salmon and top with the second piece, skin side up, put more dill sprigs on top.

4. Press the salmon well - cover it with foil or a board, and place weights on top (may use cans or jars of food). Refrigerate for 24 hours or more. This will keep approximately one week in the refrigerator.

5. Remove the dill pieces and serve fish raw (it has been cured), cut in very thin slices on the diagonal, with well-buttered rye bread, pumpernickel bread or hard bread and fresh butter (or cream fraiche or cream cheese).

DO NOT FREEZE (although you may use salmon which has been frozen and then thawed for this recipe).

The following recipes go particularly well with

Chenin Blanc, Gewurztraminer, and Dry Reisling

Some people think they don't like curry but if you don't tell them what it is, they love it. A great make-ahead dish — it gets better the next day and keeps well on a buffet table:

DAHI MURGH (INDIAN)
Chicken and Yoghurt Curry
(Serves 4)

INGREDIENTS

2 lbs	chicken breast, thighs and legs
1 1/2 tsp	salt
1/4 cup	ghee or oil
1 1/2 cups	chopped onions
3 cloves	garlic, minced
1 tsp	fresh ginger, minced
1/2 tsp	ground cumin
1 tsp	ground tumeric
1 tsp	ground coriander
1/2 to 1 tsp	ground hot red pepper
1/4 tsp	ground fennel
2	large ripe tomatoes, diced
1/4 cup	fresh coriander or mint, chopped
1/2 cup	plain yoghurt
1 1/2 tsp	garam masala
1	lemon, cut into quarters
	chopped mint or coriander leaves, for garnish

METHOD

1. Clean chicken pieces and dry and sprinkle with salt. In a large heavy fry pan, heat 1/4 cup ghee to 350 degrees, and cook the chicken for a few minutes until they are barely colored. Remove to a platter.

2. In the same pan (you may need to add a little ghee), add the onions, minced garlic and ginger and cook over moderate heat 5 to 10 minutes, until cooked to a golden color.

3. Turn heat to low and add 1/2 tsp ground cumin, 1 tsp tumeric, 1 tsp coriander, 1/2 tsp ground red pepper, 1/4 tsp fennel and cook until you can smell the aroma of the spices, stirring constantly. Add tomatoes and 1 T of fresh coriander or 2 T of chopped mint. Add yoghurt. Taste and add more coriander and salt if desired.

4. Add the chicken, turn up heat to moderate and turn chicken in the sauce. Sprinkle with garam masala. When sauce comes to just a boil, turn heat to low and cook 15 to 25 minutes until just tender.

5. If liquid from chicken is not evaporated, uncover and turn heat up, stirring. Remove to a hot platter and garnish with chopped mint or coriander, and serve with rice and chapatis, and lemon wedges to be squeezed over the curry if desired.

TO PREPARE IN A.M.: Steps 1 through 4, but undercook a bit.

TO PREPARE A DAY IN ADVANCE: Steps 1 through 4, but undercook a bit.

TO FREEZE: Steps 1 through 4, but undercook a bit, but may need to add more salt when reheating and possibly more spices.

Note: ghee is clarified butter.

"Yours was the first Chinese Chicken salad I tasted, long before it became ubiquitous. And it is still my odds-on favorite."

—Norman Lear, producer

CHINESE CHICKEN SALAD

(Serves 6)

When I used to cater the weekend screenings for Norman Lear, no matter what else we were serving, we always had to have this salad! I hope you enjoy it as much as he did.

INGREDIENTS

3-4 lb	*frying chicken or 3 large chicken breasts*
2-4 oz	*sai fun bean threads or mei fun rice noodles*
4 cups	*shredded lettuce*
1 cup	*finely chopped green onions*

Garnish:

2-4 T	*slivered almonds*
24 T	*toasted sesame seeds*
2 T	*slivered candied red ginger (optional)*

Sesame Seed Oil Dressing:

1/2 tsp	*dry mustard*
1/2 tsp	*freshly ground black pepper*
1/2 tsp	*salt or seasoned salt*

1/4 cup	salad or peanut oil
1 T	sesame seed oil
1 T	Chinese plum sauce
1 T	Hoisin Sauce
3 T	sugar
1/4 cup	white wine vinegar (or more to taste)
1/4 cup	balsamic vinegar

METHOD

1. Cook chicken (either poach, sauté, broil or bake), remove skin and bones, if any, and cut meat into slivers, or shred.

2. Combine ingredients for dressing and mix thoroughly.

3. Break or cut the rice sticks or bean threads into 3 to 4 inch pieces and drop them into hot oil (375 degrees F). (Note: the oil must be hot or they won't puff up immediately.) As soon as they puff up and crisp (about 1 second) remove and drain on a paper towel - do not brown.

4. Toss shredded chicken and green onions with half of dressing. Add lettuce and fried noodles and toss with remainder of dressing. Sprinkle with sesame seed, almonds and candied ginger and serve immediately.

TO DO IN A.M.: Steps 1, 2 and 3.

TO DO A DAY IN ADVANCE: Steps 1, 2 and 3.

TO FREEZE: Do not freeze, but can make dressing and keep in refrigerator several weeks ahead and you can freeze the cooked chicken.

Note: If you want to take this on a picnic or to a party, cook the chicken and shred and place in bottom of a bowl with some of the dressing over the chicken and green onions. Place the shredded lettuce on top — no dressing. Take the fried rice sticks or bean threads in another bowl or plastic bag. When you get where you're going mix them all with more dressing and garnish.

If you can't get rice sticks or bean threads you can cut up won ton noodles and fry them (or some markets sell them already fried) or if you're really desperate, use the canned or packaged Chinese noodles, or fry strips of flour tortillas. (What you want is something crispy.)

If this isn't the best noodle pudding you've ever had, I'd like to have your recipe:

NOODLE PUDDING

This pudding may be used as a starch with a dinner, or as a dessert.

INGREDIENTS

1/2 lb	wide noodles
1/2 lb	butter at room temperature
4	eggs at room temperature, beaten well
1 pint	sour cream
2 tsp	vanilla
4 T	sugar
1/2 tsp	ground cinnamon
1/8 tsp each	ground nutmeg, ground mace, ground cardamom
	crushed corn flakes
	coconut
	raisins

METHOD

1. Cook and drain noodles, rinse in hot water

2. Cut the butter into the noodles.

3. In a separate bowl, mix the eggs with 1 pint sour cream, 2 tsp vanilla, 4 T sugar, 1/2 tsp cinnamon, 1/8 tsp each nutmeg, mace and cardamom.

4. Mix the noodles with the sour cream mixture, and pour into a 3 quart oblong baking dish.

5. Sprinkle top with crushed corn flake crumbs and bake at 350 degrees in a pre-heated oven for 1 hour.

6. If desired, after 50 minutes of baking, add coconut and/or raisins on top and bake the remaining 10 minutes.

TO PREPARE IN MORNING: Steps 1 through 4.

TO PREPARE A DAY IN ADVANCE: Steps 1 through 4 (or 5, and reheat 10 minutes)

TO FREEZE: Steps 1 through 4.

Note: You can reduce sour cream to 1/2 pint and butter to 1/4 lb.

Recipes
to go with
Sauvignon Blanc

CRAB OR SHIMP QUICHE

INGREDIENTS

Crust:

1-1/3 cup	*flour*
1/4 lb	*sweet butter*
2 T	*cold white wine*
1/2 tsp	*salt*
1	*egg yolk*

Filling:

1 lb	*crabmeat or shrimp*
3 T	*parsley, chopped*
	salt
3	*eggs*
2 cups	*heavy cream*
3/4 lb	*Jarlsberg cheese, grated*
few drops	*Worcestershire Sauce*
6 T	*sweet butter*
1 tsp	*tarragon*
	white pepper
3	*egg yolks*
dash	*nutmeg*

METHOD

1. Sift flour and salt together. Cut in the butter. Add yolk and wine to bring dough together. Roll out and fit into 10" quiche or pie pan. Prick bottom of shell and chill while making quiche filling.

2. Sauté crabmeat or shrimp in butter. Add seasonings. Beat eggs and yolks. Add cream, nutmeg, cheese and Worcestershire. Add crabmeat or shrimp mixture to egg and cream mixture. Mix thoroughly and pour into chilled shell. Bake 10 minutes at 450 degrees. Reduce heat to 350 degrees and continue baking 30 to 40 minutes or until golden brown and puffed.

Note: Can substitute salmon or shrimp for crab or drained, chopped spinach sauted with onions for vegetarians. Can substitute half-and-half or milk for cream, but cream tastes best.

116

SALMON OR CRABMEAT MOUSSE

INGREDIENTS

1 T	*gelatin*
3 T	*cold water*
1/2 cup	*mayonnaise*
2 T	*lime juice*
2 T	*lemon juice*
1 T each	*parsley and chives, chopped*
1 T	*Dijon mustard*
	salt, pepper, seasoned salt to taste
1 slice	onion, minced fine
1 T	*sweet pickle relish*
2 cups	*flaked, cooked crabmeat or salmon*
3/4 cup	*heavy cream, whipped*

METHOD

1. Soften 1 T gelatin in 3 T cold water and dissolve it over hot water.

2. Mix gelatin with 1/4 cup mayonnaise, 2 T each lime and lemon juice, 1 T parsley and chives, 1 T Dijon mustard, seasonings, 1 slice minced onion, 1 T pickle relish.

3. Fold in 2 cups crabmeat or salmon and 3/4 cup heavy cream, whipped. Pour the mixture into a buttered ring mold or fish mold and chill until set.

4. Unmold on a chilled platter and garnish with thin slices of lime. Fill the center with avocado mashed with lime juice and sprinkled with chives.

TO PREPARE IN MORNING: Steps 1 through 4.

TO PREPARE A DAY IN ADVANCE: Steps 1 through 4.

TO FREEZE: Steps 1 through 4.

VEGETABLE TERRINE
(Serves 6 to 12)

INGREDIENTS

4 oz	Swiss cheese
1 lb	carrots
1 lb	cauliflower
1/4 lb	mushrooms
4	minced shallots
1/4 cup	minced onions
8 T	butter
1 tsp	minced tarragon
1 tsp	minced basil
2 T	parsley, minced
	salt
	pepper
1 lb	spinach, cleaned and stemmed
pinch	nutmeg
4	eggs
	water

METHOD

1. Preheat oven to 400 degrees F. Line a one-pound loaf pan (bread sized pyrex) with aluminum foil and butter well.

2. Shred Swiss cheese. Chop carrots coarsely and chop cauliflower and mushrooms coarsely and shallots and onions finely. Put into separate bowls. Heat 2 T butter in a medium fry pan and sauté carrots until tender (about 50 to 10 minutes). Put into a bowl. Add 1 tsp minced tarragon. In same fry pan, in 2 T butter, sauté cauliflower over medium heat until tender (about 5 minutes). Add 1 tsp minced basil and 2 T minced parsley. Put into another bowl. Season with salt and pepper.

3. In the same pan, in 2 T butter, sauté shallots until translucent. Add mushrooms and sauté till tender (about 2-3 minutes). Drain and add half to carrots and half to cauliflower. Season with salt and pepper.

4. In same pan, in 2 T butter, saute 1/4 cup onions until translucent. Add spinach, a little grated nutmeg and salt and pepper.

5. Beat 4 eggs till frothy then add the cheese. Divide evenly between carrot and cauliflower mixture and mix well (keep carrots and cauliflower in separate bowls).

118

6. Put cauliflower mixture in bottom of prepared pan, put drained spinach over cauliflower then carefully put carrot mixture over spinach.

7. Put the loaf pan into a larger pan and put boiling water into the larger pan about halfway up the loaf pan. Put into oven for about 45 minutes or until a knife put into center comes out clean.

8. Invert into a warm serving plate and let rest about 10 minutes. Remove the foil and slice and serve.

TO PREPARE IN A.M.: Steps 1 through 6.

TO PREPARE A DAY IN ADVANCE: Steps 1 through 6.

TO FREEZE: Best fresh, but may freeze if necessary.

Note: This may also be served cold.

Recipes to go with Roussanne & Marsanne

FRIED DUMPLINGS

INGREDIENTS

1/2 lb	bok choy or celery cabbage
1/2 lb	ground pork
1/4 lb	shrimp, ground or finely chopped, raw
1 tsp	grated fresh ginger
2 T	soy sauce
1/2 tsp	salt
2 T	sesame oil
1 T	dry sherry
1 pkg	sui mai skins or wrappers
3 T	oil
	water

METHOD

1. Clean cabbage, and trim off any wilted portions. Chop very finely. Squeeze in a clean tea towel to extract any moisture.

2. In a bowl, combine drained cabbage, pork, shrimp, 1 tsp grated ginger, 2 T soy, 1/2 tsp salt, 2 T sesame oil, and 1 T sherry.

3. Place approximately 2 tsp filling in center of wrapper, and fold into half circle, pleating and pinching the edges together. May moisten the edges with a little water to help seal.

4. Heat a frying pan with 3 T of oil, and place dumplings in a circular pattern, sealed edges up.

5. Fry over medium heat until light brown. Add water to cover the dumplings 2/3, cover and cook over medium heat until water evaporates (8-10 minutes).

6. Serve hot with pepper oil, vinegar and soy sauce, to be mixed individually as a dip.

Makes approximately 30 dumplings

TO PREPARE IN A.M.: Steps 1 through 5, but cook 5 minutes and reheat at serving time.

TO PREPARE A DAY IN ADVANCE: Steps 1 through 5, but cook 5 minutes and reheat at serving time.

TO FREEZE: Steps 1 through 5, but cook 5 minutes and reheat at serving time.

Note: If you make the dumplings ahead and wish to re-heat them, be sure to spray the pan with Pam or a similar product and use 1 or 2 T oil.

SHRIMP TOAST

INGREDIENTS

1 lb	shrimp, peeled and deveined
4	water chestnuts, chopped fine
1	scallion (green onion), chopped fine
1/2	onion, chopped fine
1/4 - 1/2 tsp	seasoned salt to taste
1 tsp	salt
1/8 tsp	ginger put thru garlic press or minced
1/2	egg
1 tsp	cornstarch
1 tsp	dry sherry
6 pieces	slightly dry bread, cut into squares or triangles, crust removed
4 cups	oil for deep frying

METHOD

1. Chop shrimp almost to a paste.
2. Chop water chestnuts, scallion and onion fine and add to shrimp and chop together. Place in a bowl.
3. Add seasoned salt, 1 tsp salt, 1/8 tsp ginger pressed, 1/2 egg, 1 tsp cornstarch, 1 tsp dry sherry and mix well.
4. Scoop approximately 1 T shrimp mixture onto the quarter piece of bread.
5. Fry at 375 degrees a few at a time. Place in the oil shrimp side down first, then turn, fry till light brown and drain.

Makes at least 24 pieces.

The mixture can be frozen by itself and spread on bread at last minute to be fried; or it can be put on bread and frozen, or can be made up completely and reheated in oven. I believe it tastes best when it is fried at the last minute.

For a buffet party, the shrimp toast may be held warm on a warming tray.

Sauvignon Blanc

Fumé Blanc

White Burgundy

SPINACH GNOCCHI

(Serves 4 to 6)

INGREDIENTS

1 lb	*ricotta cheese*
2	*eggs*
1	*egg white*
1/4 tsp	*nutmeg*
1/4 cup	*minced fresh basil leaves*
1/8 tsp	*thyme*
	zest of 1 lime or lemon
1/4 cup	*grated Parmesan cheese*
1/2 tsp	*minced garlic*
20 oz	*drained frozen chopped spinach*
	salt and pepper to taste
1/2 cup	*Wondra flour (or all purpose)*
1 bunch	*fresh spinach, cleaned*

Sauce:

4 T	*butter or olive oil*
1	*large shallot, minced*
1 T	*lemon or lime juice*
1/2 cup	*pine nuts (optional)*

METHOD

1. In a food processor, mix everything except spinach and salt and pepper. When well processed, add chopped spinach (drained well) and season to taste with salt and pepper.

2. With wet teaspoons, make little balls of the mixture and roll in flour very lightly. Put on a flat tray in the refrigerator for 20 minutes or longer.

3. In a 4 quart pot, boil water. Drop in half of the gnocchi and turn heat to simmer (don't boil) for 5 to 7 minutes, until they float to the top. Continue the same way with the remaining half of the gnocchi. Save the water.

4. In a large frying pan, heat the butter or olive oil for the sauce. Add the minced shallot and cook until it is wilted. (If using pine nuts, add them here and stir until lightly browned. Add the lemon or lime juice. Mix well. Pour the gnocchi into the sauce and turn to coat well. Serve hot.

5. In the water used to cook the gnocchi, blanch the spinach leaves just

until wilted, drain. Put the spinach on a serving plate and top with the
gnocchi.

TO PREPARE IN A.M.: Steps 1 and 2 best, but can do through 4.

TO PREPARE A DAY IN ADVANCE: Steps 1 and 2 best, but can do
through 4.

TO FREEZE: Best fresh but can do through 4.

POULET A L'ESTRAGON AU BRUN
(FRANCE)
(CHICKEN WITH TARRAGON, BROWN SAUCE)
(Serves 4)

INGREDIENTS

	breasts and legs from 3# to 4# frying chicken
1 1/2 cup	*flour*
	salt and pepper and/or seasoned salt
1/4 cup	*Cognac or Brandy*
6 T	*butter*
2 T	*vegetable oil*
3 T	*finely minced shallots*
1/4 tsp	*minced garlic*
3	*sprigs tarragon (2 tsp dry)*
1/2 cup	*dry Vermouth*
2 T	*Glacé de Viande (meat glaze)*
1 cup	*chicken stock or water*
2 tsp	*potato starch (optional)*
	watercress and 4 or more mushrooms for garnish

128

METHOD

1. Bone breasts and thighs, cut off wing tips and small bones of wings. Mix flour with salt and pepper and/or seasoned salt and lightly coat chicken.

2. In a heavy pan, heat 2 T butter and T oil. When it foams, put in the chicken and brown slowly all over. Don't crowd the pan. Pour 1/4 cup Brandy or Cognac over the chicken and cook until it almost evaporates. Remove chicken and keep warm. If necessary, add 2 T butter to pan then add minced shallots and 1/4 tsp minced garlic and saute till limp. Add 2 T finely minced fresh tarragon (or 2 tsp dried). Deglaze the pan with 1/2 cup dry Vermouth. Add 2 T glacé de viande and stir well. Add 1 cup chicken stock and reduce sauce to about half. (May strain if desired.) If you want a thicker sauce, you may add 2 tsp potato starch dissolved in water or chicken stock. Taste for seasoning and adjust accordingly. Swirl in 2 T butter.

3. Cut knobs off drumsticks and put chicken onto heatproof serving dish.

4. Pour sauce over and finish cooking in 300 degree oven, or keep warm if chicken is cooked. Garnish with watercress and sauteed mushroom caps and a few sprigs of tarragon on the chicken. May put frills on chicken legs.

TO PREPARE IN A.M.: Steps 1 through 3.

TO PREPARE A DAY IN ADVANCE: Steps 1 through 3.

TO FREEZE: Steps 1 through 3 (freezes beautifully). When reheating, don't let sauce boil — use low heat.

This Roman style chicken is a most succulent, perfect and simple way to roast a chicken:

POLLO AL LIMONE
(Chicken with Lemon)
(Serves 2 to 4)

INGREDIENTS

1	*3 to 4 lb frying chicken*
2	*lemons*
1 clove	*garlic*
5 sprigs	*oregano or basil*
	seasoned salt or salt
	pepper
	white wine

METHOD

1. Clean chicken and sprinkle with juice of one lemon, inside and out. Stuff the cavity with a whole lemon which has been punched with a fork, a cut clove of garlic and a branch or leaves of oregano or basil. Push some oregano or basil under the breast skin and thigh skin of the chicken and sprinkle the outside of the chicken with seasoned salt or salt and pepper.

2. Place the chicken on a rack, in a roasting pan, breast side down, and pour some white wine into the cavity. Preheat the oven to 350 degrees, and roast the chicken for 45 minutes.

3. Turn the chicken to breast side up and roast for an additional 15 to 20 minutes. May baste frequently with pan drippings or white wine if desired.

Chardonnay

Although shellfish is among the most expensive of fish, you may substitute firm fleshed fish for a less costly meal. For a different flavor, this could be made with chunks of chicken instead of shellfish. For an elaborate meal, you could include lobster if the pocketbook permits.

This is a truly delicious one dish meal served with a tossed green salad and a crusty bread:

NANCY'S CRAB GUMBO

INGREDIENTS

2	*onions, chopped fine*
2 T	*bacon fat (or butter)*
4 T	*flour*
2 quarts	*soup stock (chicken or fish)*
2 small cans	*tomatoes (1 lb each)*
2 lbs	*fresh okra (or frozen), sliced 1/4" thick*
1 lb	*shrimp — shell off (or on)*
1 lb	*crab (dungeness whole, cleaned and cut into pieces, or fresh or frozen crab meat)*
3 T	*parsley, chopped*
1	*bay leaf*
	salt and pepper
	cooked rice, if desired

METHOD

1. Brown onions in melted bacon fat. Add 4 T flour, 2 qts soup stock, tomatoes and okra. Cook about 2 hours.

2. Add shrimp, crab (lobster if desired) and 3 T chopped parsley, bay leaf, salt and pepper, cook about 15-20 minutes more. Be careful not to overcook seafood.

3. Serve hot in a good sized soup bowl, if desired with a small mound of rice in the center of each bowl.

TO PREPARE IN MORNING: Step 1

TO PREPARE DAY IN ADVANCE: Step 2

TO FREEZE: Steps 1 and 2, but only cook 5 minutes. Defrost and cook till hot, about 15 minutes.

This may seem lengthy, but it's really easy and a great dish for a crowd.

The only time I had as good a paella was in Spain, and it was cooked over a wood fire:

PAELLA

INGREDIENTS

2	skinned chicken breasts, cut 1/6's marinated in salt and pepper
1/4 cup	olive oil
pinch ea	cardamom, coriander
12 or more	sauteed mushrooms
2	lobsters, cut into chunks or 1 lb meat
12 or more	shrimp, peeled and deveined
1/2 cup	olive oil
2	onions, chopped
1	green pepper (sweet), chopped
1	crushed garlic clove
2 cups	Uncle Ben's rice (uncooked)
2	pimentos, sliced
pinch	oregano
pinch	cuminseed
5 cups	chicken stock
1	Italian sausage cut in pieces
1/2 lb	Canadian bacon or smoked ham, diced
1	small bottle capers, drained and rinsed
1 tsp	powdered saffron
	salt and pepper, or seasoned salt to taste
1 cup	green beans
1 cup	green peas
12 or more	artichoke hearts
12 or more	clams or oysters, raw, in shell (optional)

METHOD

1. Cut skinned chicken breasts into 6 pieces each, marinate overnight in pinch each of salt and pepper, 1/4 cup olive oil, pinch of cardamom and a pinch of coriander.

2. Drain chicken from olive oil. In a large frying pan or paella pan, heat the

134

drained olive oil and saute chicken. Remove chicken. In same pan, saute mushrooms, remove, saute lobster chunks just until they turn red or are just cooked, then remove. Saute shrimps and remove (or may use already cooked shrimps). May need to add more oil at times.

3. In 1/2 cup olive oil, saute 2 chopped onions and chopped green pepper and 1 crushed garlic clove, until the onion is golden. Stir in the 2 cups o f raw rice and cook it, stirring, until the grains are coated with oil. Stir in 1 pimento, sliced, and a pinch each of oregano and cuminseed.

3a. Add 5 cups chicken stock, 1 Italian sausage, cut into pieces, 1/2 pound Canadian bacon or ham, diced, 1 small bottle capers, drained, 1 tsp powdered saffron, a few ground peppercorns, and salt to taste.

   * If using clams and/or oysters, add them here. Cover, and cook 20-25 minutes, or until rice is tender and liquid is absorbed.

4. Add 1 cup each beans and peas, and cook 5 minutes.

5. Stir in lobster, chicken, and 1 sliced pimento, into the rice mixture. Arrange the paella on a large serving dish, or serve right from the paella pan, and surround the top with a ring of artichoke hearts and cooked peeled shrimp. Put a sauteed mushroom on each artichoke.

TO PREPARE IN A.M.: Steps 1 through 3a. May need to add a little more liquid and cook more than 5 minutes to heat thoroughly.

TO PREPARE A DAY IN ADVANCE: Steps 1 through 3. Next day proceed with 3a.

TO FREEZE: Best not frozen.

SANGRIA:

Mix 1 bottle (5th or qt) wine (dry red or white) with 2/3 cup lemon juice, 1/4 cup orange juice, 1/2 cup sugar and sliced fruit (oranges, peaches, lemons, nectarines, etc.). Just before serving, add 10 to 12 oz sparkling soda water. Fill glasses with ice, and pour wine mixture over. May garnish with mint leaves also.

So simple to make and so elegant!

EMERALD SHRIMP OR EMERALD FISH

(Serves 2 to 4)

INGREDIENTS

1 lb	shrimp or fish (Salmon or white fish)
	butter or oil
1 to 2	cloves garlic, mashed
	seasoned salt
10 oz	frozen chopped spinach
2 T	minced shallots
pinch	nutmeg
1/2 cup or more	whipping cream or yogurt
1 T	basil, dill, or tarragon
	salt and pepper

METHOD

1. Peel and devein shrimp.
2. In a frying pan, heat about 2 T butter or oil and saute garlic just until you

can smell it. Add 1/4 tsp seasoned salt, then add shrimp and saute just until color changes to pink. (Do not overcook.) Remove from pan.

3. Defrost spinach. In the same pan, saute the shallot in 2 T butter or oil. When they are translucent, add the spinach, nutmeg and a sprinkle of seasoned salt. Put 1/2 cup cream in a blender or food processor and add 1 T of basil or dill or tarragon. Add spinach mixture and blend well. Taste for seasoning and if necessary add more cream or yogurt.

4. Put shrimps back into pan, cover with spinach mixture, mix well and heat. Serve hot. (Note: Shrimps can be heated in microwave oven, or can be put in casserole and heated in oven. If done in oven, be careful to heat quickly, so spinach doesn't lose nice green color.)

TO PREPARE IN A.M.: Steps 1 through 3.

TO PREPARE A DAY IN ADVANCE: Steps 1 through 3, but better done the same day.

TO FREEZE: Steps 1 through 3, but better done the same day.

Robert Klein's absolute favorite:

BASTILA (OR BISTEEYA) (MOROCCO)
(Serves 6 to 10, or 12 as part of Moroccan dinner)

INGREDIENTS

4	squabs or 4 lbs frying chicken cut up, with giblets; cleaned
1	large clove garlic, peeled
	salt
1 cup	chopped parsley
1 tsp	finely chopped fresh cilantro
1 cup	minced onion
1/8 tsp	pulverized saffron
1/4 tsp	ground tumeric
3/4 tsp	freshly ground black pepper
1/8 tsp	cayenne
3/4 tsp	ground ginger
1/8 tsp	cumin
3	cinnamon sticks
1 cup	butter
	salt
3 cups	water
1/4 cup	salad oil
3/4 lb - 1 lb	blanched almonds
	confectioners' sugar
	ground cinnamon
1/4 cup	lemon juice
8	large or extra large eggs
1/2-3/4 lb	phyllo pastry or strudel leaves

METHOD

1. Clean and peel garlic. Sprinkle poultry with salt. Put poultry in a casserole (at least 5 qt) with the giblets, parsley, cilantro, minced onion, 1/8 tsp saffron, 1/4 tsp tumeric, 3/4 tsp freshly ground pepper, 1/8 tsp cayenne, 3/4 tsp ground ginger, 1/8 tsp cumin, 3 cinnamon sticks, 1/2 cup (2 sticks) butter, a pinch of salt, and 3 cups water. Bring to a boil, lower heat, simmer for 1 hour covered.

2. In a 10 or 12 inch skillet heat 1/4 cup salad oil and brown the almonds

lightly. Drain well on paper towels and when they are cool, crush until coarse, or grind them. Combine with 1/3 cup confectioners' sugar and 11/2 to 2 tsp ground cinnamon. Set aside.

3. Remove poultry, giblets, cinnamon sticks and bones from casserole and put aside. Boil the sauce remaining in the casserole rapidly, uncovered, reducing the sauce to approximately 1-3/4 cups, then add 1/4 cup lemon juice. Beat the eggs till frothy, then pour them into the simmering sauce and stir continuously until the eggs cook and congeal. (They will become curdy, stiff and dry.) Put the egg mixture into a colander and drain (to ensure against a soggy bastila). Taste for salt. Set aside.

4. Remove all bones from poultry and shred meat into 11/2" pieces, and chop giblets coarsely.

5. Heat the remaining 1 cup (2 sticks) butter. When foam subsides, clarify it by pouring off clear liquid butter into a small bowl and discarding milky solids.

6. Preheat oven to 425 degrees. Unroll the filo dough, keeping them under a damp towel so they won't dry out. Brush some of the clarified butter over the bottom and sides of a 13" cake pan or sautesse pan or paella pan, then cover the bottom of the pan with one sheet of filo. Arrange 6 overlapping sheets of filo in a circle — cover the entire bottom of the pan. Brush the extended leaves with butter so they do not dry out.

7. Place chunks of poultry and giblets around edges of the pan and work toward center so that pastry is covered with a layer of shredded poultry. Cover the poultry layer with the drained egg mixture from step 3. (You may optionally put 2 to 4 baked or fried pastry leaves on top of the egg mixture.)

8. Sprinkle the almond-sugar-cinnamon mixture over the egg or pastry. Cover with all but 2 of the remaining pastry leaves, brushing each lightly with butter.

9. Fold the overlapping leaves in over the top to cover the pie, brushing each again with butter, one at a time, and fold neatly under the pie like tucking in sheets. Pour any remaining butter around the edge.

10. Bake the pie in a 425 degree oven until the top pastry leaves are golden brown, about 20 minutes for a shallow pie, to 40 minutes for a thick pie. Shake the pan to loosen the pie and run a spatula round the edges. Pour off any excess butter and save. Invert the pie onto a large, buttered baking sheet with sides. Brush the pie with the reserved butter and return to the oven to continue baking another 10 to 15 minutes, or until golden brown.

11. Remove the pie from the oven. Tilt to pour off any excess butter. Put a serving plate over the pie, and holding it firmly, invert. Dust the top of the pie with confectioners' sugar and run criss-crossing lines of cinnamon over the top. Serve very hot.

Note: The pie may be fried on top of the stove instead of baked, but if it is fried, fill first with almond mixture so that when it is inverted the almonds will be on top. The pie is traditionally served with the almond mixture on the top.

TO PREPARE IN A.M.: Steps 1 through 5 or Steps 1 through 9 (don't preheat oven in step #6 until ready to cook).

TO PREPARE A DAY IN ADVANCE: Steps 1 through 5 or Steps 1 through 9 (don't preheat oven in step #6 until ready to cook).

TO FREEZE: Steps 1 through 5 or Steps 1 through 9 (don't preheat oven in step #6 until ready to cook).

Grenache
Gamay

SOUTH PACIFIC
ROAST PORK TENDERLOIN
(Serves 4 as entry or 8 appetizer)

INGREDIENTS

1 piece	*star anise*
1/8 tsp	*five spice powder*
1/2 cup	*honey*
1 clove	*garlic, crushed*
1/8 tsp	*white pepper*
1/4 cup	*catsup*
1/4 cup	*soy sauce*
1 T	*brandy (apricot)*
2	*pork tenderloins, about 1/2 lb each*

METHOD

1. Mix star anise, 1/8 tsp five spice powder, 1/2 cup honey, garlic, 1/8 tsp white pepper, 1/4 cup catsup, 1/4 cup soy sauce and 1 T brandy.

2. Put pork into plastic bag, shallow dish, or seal-tight plastic container and pour over marinade. Marinate 3 hours, or overnight in refrigerator, turning occasionally.

3. Line a shallow pan with foil and place drained pork side by side in pan. Roast at 400 degrees F for 25 minutes. Turn the pork over, brush with marinade and roast 20 minutes more.

4. Brush generously with marinade again and return to oven 5 to 10 minutes more.

5. Slice pork very thin across grain and serve as appetizer or main dish, either hot, at room temperature, or cold. Serve with hot mustard (dry mustard mixed to a paste with water, sherry or beer just before serving).

TO PREPARE IN A.M.: Steps 1 and 2 (may include 3). If serving cold, 1 through 5.

TO PREPARE A DAY IN ADVANCE: Steps 1 and 2 (may include 3). If serving cold, 1 through 5.

TO FREEZE: Steps 1 through 5, but don't store more than 1 or 2 months — loses flavor.

BBQ SHORT RIBS - KAHLBI KUI (KOREA)

(Serves 6 to 8)

INGREDIENTS

4 lbs	meaty short ribs (lean)
	salt
2 T	brown sugar
1/3 cup	soy sauce
2 T	Sherry or rice wine
1 T	sesame seed oil
2 T	brown sugar or honey
3 cloves	garlic, minced
1/2 tsp	minced fresh ginger
2	minced green onions
1 T	toasted sesame seeds
	dash of cayenne

METHOD

1. Cut as much fat off the ribs as possible. Score the ribs at half inch intervals lengthwise and crosswise to a depth of about one half inch. Do the same to the sides. Cut the membrane along the length of the back of the bone with a sharp knife. Sprinkle the ribs with salt and rub in the brown sugar. Let stand one hour or more.

2. Mix the rest of the ingredients and marinate 1 hour or more.

3. Broil over charcoal 5 to 10 minutes, or in the oven 7 to 15 minutes.

4. Serve hot.

TO PREPARE IN A.M.: Steps 1 and 2.

TO PREPARE A DAY IN ADVANCE: Steps 1 (and step 2 if you like an intense flavor).

TO FREEZE: Steps 1 through 3 and reheat.

Beaujolais

These Frikadeller disappear almost as soon as they're out of the pan. We don't usually bother with the sauce — they're so good — hot or cold. Great as leftovers for sandwiches. Can be made with ground turkey:

FRIKADELLER (DANISH MEATBALLS)
(SERVES 6)

INGREDIENTS

2 lbs	ground meat (veal & pork)
1 to 2	onions, minced
2	eggs
1/2 to 1 cup	bread crumbs
6-12 oz	soda water or beer
1/4 tsp	freshly ground pepper
1/4 tsp	allspice, ground
1/8 tsp	nutmeg, ground
	salt to taste
	flour
	butter or olive oil

METHOD

1. In a large bowl mix all but flour and butter (may be a bit loose).

2. Make oval patties (dip your hands in cold water to make it easier) of the meat mixture and dip into flour and let sit for a few minutes.

3. In a large frying pan (Teflon if possible) melt the butter or olive oil, and when it is hot, fry the frikadeller. Serve hot plain or with sauce.

4. Serve with or without Horseradish sauce, mushroom sauce or simple gravy.

TO PREPARE IN A.M.: Steps 1 and 2.

TO PREPARE A DAY IN ADVANCE: Steps 1 and 2.

TO FREEZE: Steps 1 through 3.

(Note: If you have leftovers, these make very good cold or hot sandwiches.)

HORSERADISH SAUCE (PEBERRODSSAUCE)

Whip 8 oz whipping cream until stiff, beat in 2 T grated fresh horse-radish.

MUSHROOM SAUCE (CHAMPIGNONNSSAUCE)

1 lb	*sliced mushrooms*
2 cup	*milk*
4 T	*butter*
2 T	*Worcestershire sauce*
4 T	*flour*
1/2 tsp	*dry mustard*
	salt and pepper

METHOD

1. Brown mushrooms in the butter, sprinkle with flour and salt and pepper. Add milk slowly when the flour begins to brown. Season with Worcestershire sauce and mustard. Stir until thick and smooth.

SIMPLE GRAVY

To the drippings in the pan, add 3 T flour and brown. Add 1-1/2 cup broth (either chicken or beef or veal). Season with seasoned salt or salt and pepper. May add 1/4 cup wine or 1/2 to 1 cup sour cream and stir until smooth.

Merlot

CANARD AU POIVRE VERTE (FRANCE)
DUCK WITH GREEN PEPPERCORNS

(Serves 1 or 2)

INGREDIENTS

1	whole duck breast
	seasoned salt
1 T	crushed green peppercorns
1 T	light olive oil
1 T	butter
1	large shallot, minced
1/4 cup	Armagnac (or Brandy)
1/4 cup	duck, chicken or veal stock
1 T	glace de viande (optional)
2 T	cream
1 T	butter

METHOD

1. Season the duck with seasoned salt and the crushed green peppercorns.

2. Heat the oil and butter in a large skillet (or use Teflon and no oil), and cook both sides of duck until rare. Remove to a serving plate and keep warm. Pour off all but 1 T fat from pan and saute shallots until translucent.

3. Add the Armagnac to the skillet and scrape up all the bits in the skillet. Heat and flame. Stir in the stock, glace de viande, and cream and heat just to the boiling point and reduce by half.

4. Stir in the 1 T butter and pour over the duck and serve hot.

TO PREPARE IN A.M.: Step 1.

A quick to cook, festive dinner: Leg of Lamb Granada with pan roasted potatoes, Green Beans Echalote, Fresh Peaches in Grand Marnier.

LEG OF LAMB GRANADA
(Serves 6)

INGREDIENTS

1	*leg of lamb about 5 to 6 lbs*
about 1/4 cup	*fresh thyme or tarragon*
about 1/4 cup	*pomegranate jelly (may use red currant)*
about 2 tsp	*seasoned salt*
	fresh ground pepper
2 cloves	*garlic*
1/2 to 1 cup	*port wine*
3 or more	*potatoes, quartered*

METHOD

1. Trim fat off leg of lamb.

2. Make incisions in lamb and poke pieces of herbs into holes about every 2 inches all over meat. Put on a rack on a greased roasting pan.

3. Smear with a thin layer of pomegranate (or currant) jelly, then sprinkle with seasoned salt, pepper and pressed or minced garlic — all over.

4. Place quartered scrubbed potatoes in roasting pan, under lamb.

5. Pour about 1/2 cup wine over roast and potatoes.

6. Preheat oven to 325 degrees F and roast 18 to 25 minutes per pound. Baste every 20 minutes with wine and pan juices. When done, let rest in oven about 15 minutes before carving, so juices won't run out. Serve hot.

Note: This same method may be used with saddle of lamb, loin of lamb, or rack of lamb.

TO PREPARE IN A.M.: Steps 1 through 5 and refrigerate.

TO PREPARE A DAY IN ADVANCE: Steps 1 through 3 and refrigerate.

TO FREEZE: May freeze leftovers if there are any, but not as good reheated as fresh. Better to use leftovers for sandwiches.

Chianti

This meat sauce, which probably originated in the Ligurian region of Italy, is often used in lasagna and over hearty type pastas. It freezes very well.

MEAT SAUCE

INGREDIENTS

4	onions, minced
4 cloves	garlic, minced
2 lbs	ground meat (beef, pork)
8 oz	Italian sausage
4 oz	minced parsley
4 qts	crushed tomatoes
16 oz	tomato sauce
6 oz	tomato paste
1 or 2	dried hot peppers
4 T	minced oregano
	seasoned salt or salt
	pepper
1 lb	mushrooms, sliced
1 cup	dry red wine
4 oz	grated Parmesan cheese

Enough for 2 to 4 lbs of Pasta

METHOD

1. In a large pot, heat a little olive oil and saute onions and garlic. When onions are soft, add meat and sausage. When sausage and meat are no longer pink, add parsley, tomatoes, tomato sauce and paste and all seasonings mix well, add mushrooms and let cook a few hours. About a half hour before it's finished, add the dry red wine and grated Parmesan cheese. Stir well.

This is best if refrigerated overnight, then the fat congeals and can be removed easily.

Note: If desired, meat can be replaced with ground turkey or ground chicken.

A terrific casserole dish which freezes beautifully before or after baking, and can be doubled, tripled, etc. easily:

MELANZANA (EGGPLANT) PARMIGIANA
(Serves 4 to 6)

INGREDIENTS
1	*large eggplant*
	salt
	flour
	olive oil
	pepper
2 cups	*marinara sauce*
1/2 cup	*grated Parmesan cheese*
8 oz	*sliced Mozzarella cheese*

METHOD
1. Peel eggplant, if desired, and cut in slices about 1/4 to 1/3 inch thick. Salt them and let them stand for an hour, drain off liquid and pat dry. Dip each slice in flour and saute slowly in olive oil until golden on each side. Drain well.

2. In a shallow greased baking dish (3 quart Pyrex is good), place a layer of cooked eggplant, season with pepper, cover with some marinara sauce, some grated Parmesan and slices of Mozzarella cheese. Repeat for 1 more layer. Place in a preheated 250 degree F oven approximately 30 minutes, or until cheese is melted.

This sauce probably originated around the Naples area of Italy. Today it is used all over Italy, over pasta, vegetables and as part of other sauces. This recipe makes approximately 1 quart, and freezes well:

SALSA MARINARA

INGREDIENTS

1 T	olive oil (or more)
1	small onion, minced
1 to 3 cloves	garlic, minced or pressed
4 cups	canned whole or crushed tomatoes
1 T	fresh basil, minced
1 T	fresh oregano, minced
	seasoned slat or salt to taste
	pepper to taste

METHOD

1. In 1 or more T oil, saute the minced onion and garlic until the onion is transparent. Add the crushed tomatoes and the basil and oregano and seasoned salt or salt and pepper to taste, and simmer a minimum of 10 minutes.

You may use fresh tomatoes, peeled and seeded and chopped to replace the same amount of canned tomatoes if you wish.

History has it that this is called Harlot's sauce because it is so quick to make (between tricks). It originated in the region of Naples.

SALSA ALA MERETRICE
(HARLOT'S SAUCE)

INGREDIENTS

4 T	olive oil
4 T	butter
3 lg cloves	garlic, minced
2	anchovies, minced
1/2 cup	chopped black olives
4	green olives, chopped
1 T	oregano
1/4 tsp	pepper, coarse ground black
1/8 tsp	ground red pepper
1 T	basil
1 cup	fresh tomatoes chopped, peeled
4 T	grated Parmesan cheese
	minced parsley

METHOD

1. Heat oil and butter in a large skillet and saute minced garlic about 2 minutes over medium low heat. Add anchovies and olives, oregano, black pepper and ground red pepper and simmer about 10 to 20 minutes.

2. Add basil and tomatoes and grated Parmesan cheese and simmer 5 minutes. Add 2 to 4 T minced parsley just before serving.

Serve over one pound of cooked spaghetti, accompanied by a bowl of grated Parmesan or Romano cheese.

This recipe is popular in San Francisco, and was created by Italian fishermen who had immigrated to the area. It's delicious and very easy to make:

CIOPPINO

ITALIAN FISHERMEN'S STEW
(Serves 6)

EQUIPMENT
One	*8qt pot with lid*
One	*6qt pot with lid*

INGREDIENTS
2 lbs	*fresh littleneck clams*
2 lbs	*fresh mussels*
1 lb	*raw shrimp*
1 to 2	*cooked crabs*
3	*onions, chopped*
6 cloves	*garlic, minced or pressed*
3 T	*olive oil*
2 cups	*tomato sauce*
1-1/2 cup	*tomato paste*
2 cups	*water*
1 T	*basil*
1 T	*oregano*
	seasoned salt or salt and pepper to taste

METHOD
1. Clean all the fish. Saute the onion and garlic in the olive oil in the 8 qt pot until the onions are soft. Add the tomato sauce, tomato paste, water, wine and seasonings. Simmer the sauce for one hour.

2. Meanwhile, put 1 cup of water into the 6 qt pot and bring the water to a boil. Add the clams and mussels and put the cover on the pan. Continue to cook over medium high heat about 8 minutes until the clams and mussels have opened. Shake the pan once or twice during cooking. Remove from heat and leave lid on.

3. Add shrimp to sauce, simmer about 5 minutes with lid on then add crab, clams and mussels. Simmer another 5 minutes with lid on.

Serve in large soup plates with lots of French bread.

Note: To cook the live crab: In a large pot, bring about 8 qts water to a boil with 2 T salt. Grasp live crab from rear and drop into boiling water. Cover kettle and simmer 20 to 25 minutes after water returns to boil. Lift out crabs with tongs and let cool.

This light dish from the Roman region of Italy is simple to prepare and good for family or company:

VEAL PICCATA
(Serves 4 to 6)

INGREDIENTS

1 1/2 lb	thin slices veal scallops
	salt or seasoned salt
	freshly ground pepper
	all purpose flour
4 T	clarified butter
2 T	minced shallots
4 T	chicken or veal stock
3 T	lemon juice (or more to taste)
4 T	minced parsley
	lemon slices

METHOD

1. Pound the veal lightly. Sprinkle with salt or seasoned salt, pepper, and dredge lightly in flour.

2. Heat the butter in a large skillet and brown the veal quickly and lightly over moderate to high heat, turning once. Cook a small amount at a time so as not to crowd the pan, or the veal with stew, not brown. Use more butter if necessary. Transfer the cooked meat to a warm serving platter and keep warm.

3. After all meat is cooked, pour off most of the butter from the skillet, and in the remaining (about 2 T butter), cook the 2 T minced shallots until just limp, then add 4 T chicken or veal stock (or water or dry white wine) and swirl it around, scraping the bottom and sides of the skillet to loosen the brown particles. Add 3 T (or more to taste) of lemon juice.

4. Pour the sauce over the meat and sprinkle with parsley and garnish the platter with lemon slices and parsley.

Zinfandel

This takes a bit of time, but freezes beautifully for later meals:

MY FAVORITE STUFFED CABBAGE
(Serves 10)

INGREDIENTS

20	*whole outside cabbage leaves*
2-1/2 lbs	*ground beef*
1-1/4 cup	*cooked rice*
1	*large onion, chopped*
2-1/2 T	*sugar*
2	*large eggs*
1/2 tsp	*garlic powder*
	salt to taste
	pepper to taste
	seasoned salt to taste
7-1/2 cups	*cooked tomatoes (canned)*
1 cup	*raisins*
3/4 cup	*crushed ginger snaps*
1/2 cup	*lemon juice*
5 T	*brown sugar*

METHOD

1. Remove hearts from 2-3 cabbages, and blanch in boiling water 5 minutes or more. Remove 20 whole large outer leaves.

2. In a bowl, combine 2-1/2 lbs ground beef, 11/4 cups cooked rice, 1 large finely chopped onion, 21/2 T sugar, 2 large eggs, 1/2 tsp garlic powder and salt, pepper and seasoned salt to taste, and mix well. Mixture should be soft and moist.

3. Divide filling among leaves and roll each leaf.

4. Shred cabbage heart and inside leaves which you haven't used, and line a casserole or baking pan with half the shredded cabbage. Lay the stuffed cabbage leaves on top and cover with the remaining shredded cabbage.

5. Combine 7-1/2 cups tomatoes, 1 cup raisins, 3/4 cup crushed ginger snaps, 1/2 cup lemon juice, 5 T brown sugar and 1/2 tsp salt. Pour over stuffed cabbage. Simmer 21/2 - 3 hours, or till done. Taste for seasoning, and if necessary, add more seasoned salt or salt and pepper this may be simmered on top of the stove or put in the oven at 350 degrees.

TO PREPARE IN A.M.: Steps 1 through 5.

TO PREPARE A DAY IN ADVANCE: Steps 1 through 5.

TO FREEZE: Steps 1 through 5. To serve, defrost and reheat.

This is traditionally served with rice — either plain boiled or pilaf. (You need something to sop up the delicious sauce.)

Note: An easy way to prepare the cabbage is to freeze it for 8 hrs. or more. You can then separate the leaves without the bother of blanching.

Pinot Noir

Nice for an easy BBQ (or broil):
SHISH KEBAB (MID EASTERN)
(Serves 4 to 6)

INGREDIENTS

2 lbs	boned leg of lamb or beef cut into 1" or 2" cubes
2 T	olive oil
2 T	lemon juice
2 T	dry wine
1 tsp	crushed oregano leaves
1 tsp	crushed thyme leaves
6	long skewers
2	green or red sweet peppers cut into 2" squares

12	*raw mushrooms, cleaned*
12	*pearl onions, peeled*
6	*cherry tomatoes*

METHOD

1. Preheat broiler or barbeque (start fire 1 hour in advance if using charcoal).

2. Put meat in a bowl, add 2 T olive oil, 2 T lemon juice, 2 T dry wine, minced onion, garlic clove, salt, pepper and seasoned salt, 1 tsp oregano and 1 tsp thyme. Mix well, cover and let stand at room temperature 2 hours, or in refrigerator 4 to 6 hours. Bring to room temperature 2 hours before cooking.

3. Alternate the meat on the skewers with peppers, mushrooms and onions. Broil the kebabs approximately 5 minutes on each side, 3 to 4 inches from heat, until the meat is done to your taste. Put a cherry tomato on the end of each skewer and serve, or place in broiler or over charcoal for another minute to cook tomato.

Serve with a pilaf or Tabooli.

TO PREPARE IN A.M.: Step 2.

TO PREPARE A DAY IN ADVANCE: Step 2, but will have very strong flavor of marinade.

TO FREEZE: Step 2.

Delicious on a cold night — hearty enough for a main dish:

RUSSIAN CABBAGE BORSCH (OR BORSCHT)

INGREDIENTS

2-1/2 lbs	beef shank (or chuck and 2 marrow bones)
2	onions, chopped
1/2 clove	garlic, pressed or minced
1 T	salt
1/2 T	pepper
6 cups	water or beef broth
2	carrots, sliced
2 cups	crushed canned tomatoes
1-1 lb	can sliced or julienned beets (or 3 large fresh)
2	medium potatoes, peeled and cubed
1	small head or 2 cups finely shredded cabbage
	juice of 3 lemons (1/2 cup)
2-3 T	sugar, or to taste
	(sour cream if desired)

METHOD

1. Place beef (bones if used), onions, garlic, salt, 1/2 T pepper, and 6 cups water or beef broth in a deep soup pot, cover and bring to a boil. Skim off film which rises to the top, recover and cook over low heat 30 minutes.

2. Add sliced carrots, cover and cook another 30 minutes.

3. Remove bones but keep any marrow you may have and return marrow to pot, or put it on crackers and eat as an appetizer — yum.

4. Add 2 cups crushed tomatoes, beets (either julienned, shredded or sliced), cubed potatoes and shredded cabbage. Cover and cook until potatoes are tender, about 30 minutes.

5. Add lemon juice and sugar to taste; cook 5 minutes.

6. Before serving, remove meat and cut up; return to pot.

7. Serve very hot in soup plates, accompanied by sour cream. Serves 6, generously.

THIS MAY BE FROZEN WITHOUT SOUR CREAM, OR IT KEEPS ABOUT ONE WEEK IN THE REFRIGERATOR. IT'S EVEN BETTER THE SECOND OR THIRD DAY.

This is the best tortilla soup I've ever tasted:

TORTILLA SOUP

INGREDIENTS

2 T	peanut oil
1	large onion, minced
2	shallots, minced
2 cloves	garlic, minced or pressed
1 T	cumin, ground
1	bay leaf
1 T	chili blend powder
1 T	ground coriander
1 tsp	dried or fresh cilantro
1/2 cup	minced green onions
1 tsp	dried basil
1	dried pasilla chili
1 tsp	oregano
1 qt	chicken stock
1 qt	beef stock
16 oz	diced tomatoes (canned)
16 oz	corn
1	red bell pepper, minced
	fried tortilla strips
1	avocado sliced
	shredded Jack or Swiss cheese
	shrimp or chicken, cooked

METHOD

1. In 2 T oil, saute onion until translucent, then add shallots and garlic and cook a minute. Add cumin, bay leaf, chili powder, coriander and saute until you can smell the spices. Add the cilantro, green onions, basil and pasilla chili (which has been toasted, seeded and minced) and oregano. Stir well. Add the chicken and beef stock and tomatoes, corn and bell pepper. Cook 20 minutes to 1 hour, until flavors have been well blended.

2. When ready to serve, place some tortilla strips, slices of avocado, shredded cheese, and optionally, some shrimp or chicken pieces in the soup bowl, and ladle very hot soup over. Serve immediately.

TO PREPARE IN A.M.: Step 1.

TO PREPARE A DAY IN ADVANCE: Step 1.

TO FREEZE: Step 1.

SOUP A L'OIGNON
(FRENCH ONION SOUP)
(Serves 6 to 8)

INGREDIENTS

4 T	butter, oil or poultry fat
6	large onions, sliced thinly in rounds
2	leeks, white and light green parts thinly sliced
6	shallots, thinly sliced
4 cups	beef stock
4 cups	chicken stock
1	bay leaf
2 cloves	garlic, mashed or pressed
	salt and freshly ground pepper to taste
1/2 cup	dry white or red wine, optional
2 to 4 T	cognac
6 to 8	toasted french bread rounds
	grated Gruyere cheese
	grated Parmesan cheese

METHOD

1. In a large soup pot, heat butter or fat and saute onions, leeks and shallots until golden brown, stirring frequently — be patient, it takes a long time (you may sprinkle with up to 2 T sugar to hasten browning time).

2. Add 8 cups stock and 1 bay leaf, 2 cloves garlic, salt and pepper to taste and 1/2 cup wine, if desired, and cook 1 to 2 hours.

3. About 1/2 hour before serving, add 2 to 4 T cognac, if desired.

4. Toast 6 to 8 rounds of french bread. Put them in the bottom of individual soup bowls, or large tureen, and top with grated Gruyere cheese. Remove the bay leaf from soup and pour the hot soup over the toast, sprinkle with grated Parmesan cheese, if desired, and serve immediately.

TO PREPARE IN A.M.: Steps 1 through 3.

TO PREPARE A DAY IN ADVANCE: Steps 1 through 3.

STEAK AU POIVRE VERTE (FRANCE) (GREEN PEPPER STEAK)

(Serves 4)

INGREDIENTS

2 lb	steak (top sirloin, NY or filet Mignon)
	seasoned salt to taste
1 T	crushed green peppercorns
2 T	light olive oil
2 T	butter
1/4 cup	Armagnac
1/2 cup	Creme Fraiche or heavy cream

METHOD

1. Season the steak with seasoned salt and the crushed green peppercorns.

2. Heat the oil and butter in a large skillet and cook both sides. Remove to a serving plate and keep hot.

3. Add the Armagnac to the skillet and scrape up the bits in the skillet. Heat and flame. Stir in the creme fraiche or cream, heat just to the boiling point and reduce by half.

4. Pour the sauce over the steak and serve sizzling.

TO PREPARE IN A.M.: Step 1.

TO PREPARE A DAY IN ADVANCE: Step 1.

TO FREEZE: Best not frozen.

(For creme fraiche: use 1 tsp of buttermilk for each cup of heavy cream. Heat in a saucepan until lukewarm (85F), pour into a glass and let stand at room temperature until it thickens (temperature should be between 60F and 85F). In hot weather, may take 6 hours; in cold, may take as long as 36 hours. Keeps in refrigerator about a week.)

Bordeaux and Cabernet Sauvignon

FAJITAS
(GRILLED, BROILED OR BBQ'D STEAK)
(Serves 4)

INGREDIENTS
Marinade:

1/4 cup	Tequila
1 to 2 T	lemon juice
1/4 tsp/more	cumin, ground
1/2 tsp	cilantro, minced
1 T	minced fresh basil
2 shakes	Tabasco sauce
1/2 tsp	Worcestershire sauce
1/4 tsp	pickapeppa sauce (optional)
1 tsp	seasoning, no salt or seasoned salt
3	large onions, sliced, cooked golden
1-1/2 lbs	steak (skirt, flank, top sirloin, chuck, etc.), cut 1x11/2x1/4"
8	young green onions, cleaned
1	bell pepper, cut into 10" squares or thin strips
1	tomato, firm, cut into large chunks
	tortillas (wheat, flour or corn)

Pico de Gallo sauce
guacamole
sour cream
peanut oil for frying or grilling

METHOD

1. In a large bowl, mix marinade ingredients well. Add slices of steak and let marinate a few hours (or overnight in the refrigerator). Cook onions.

2. Prepare vegetables, cover tortillas with foil to heat, make Pico de Gallo sauce and guacamole.

3. In a large frying pan, grill or sauteuese pan, heat peanut oil till very hot. Throw in the young green onions, then the meat, and toss well. Add the pepper and tomato and the cooked onions and cook only until very hot.

4. To serve, take a hot tortilla, put some steak and vegetable mixture in the tortilla, sprinkle with Pico de Gallo, some guacamole and some sour cream, and fold up like a burrito and eat.

Note: The meat can be BBQ'd in whole steaks (after marinating) and then cut into strips and eaten with or without the cooked vegetables.

Pico de Gallo:

In a bowl, mix together: 3 to 4 minced firm, ripe tomatoes, unpeeled; 1 to 2 minced seedless Serrano or Jalapeno chiles; 1 to 2 T minced fresh cilantro; 1 small minced onion. Let sit at least 20 minutes to blend flavors, salt to taste.

Guacamole:

In a bowl, mix together: 3 to 4 avacadoes, mashed; juice of half a lemon; 1/2 an onion, finely minced; 1 clove garlic, minced or pressed; 1 tomato, minced; Tabasco sauce or ffresh hot peppers, minced, to taste; minced fresh cilantro (2 to 4 sprigs), optional; seasoned salt to taste; Pickapeppa Sauce, optional, to taste. Refrigerate with an avacado pit in the center — supposed to keep from blackening.

TO PREPARE IN A.M.: Steps 1 and 2.
TO PREPARE A DAY IN ADVANCE: Step 1.
TO FREEZE: No.

RACK OF LAMB,
SADDLE OF LAMB OR LEG OF LAMB
(Allow 1/3 to 1/2 lb boneless meat per person)

INGREDIENTS

4 to 6 lbs	lamb roast
1 to 2 cloves	garlic, sliced
1/2 cup	dry Vermouth
4 T	butter or olive oil
1/4 cup	bread crumbs
1/4 cup	chopped parsley
1 clove	minced garlic or 2 shallots
	salt
	fresh ground pepper
2 tsp	(fresh) oregano
1 tsp	thyme
1/2 tsp	Herbs de Provence

METHOD: Bring roast to room temperature:

1. Poke slivers of garlic into the lamb roast, after removing excess fat, leaving only 1/4" of fat to cover meat.

2. Pour 1/2 cup dry Vermouth over roast and let sit 1 hour, or overnight in refrigerator.

3. Mix remaining ingredients — 4 T butter or olive oil, 1/4 cup bread crumbs, 1/4 cup chopped parsley, 1 clove minced garlic or 2 minced shallots, salt and pepper, 2 tsp oregano, 1 tsp thyme and 1/2 tsp Herbs de Province — a food processor is perfect for this job.

4. With meat at room temperature, spread ingredients of step 3 over the roast and put into a 325 degree oven for 20 minutes per pound, or until done to your preference. Baste from time to time with more Vermouth, if desired. Lamb is best if it's slightly pink. (The French way of roasting racks or saddles of lamb is to salt and pepper them, roast in preheated 450 degree oven for 10 to 20 minutes, then lower heat to 350 degrees, spread with persillade (ingredients in step 3), and cook another 30 to 45 minutes.) Let rest 10 to 15 minutes before carving. (The longer time for leg of lamb.)

Note: This is very nice with pan roasted new potatoes and a vegetable of your choice.

TO PREPARE IN A.M.: Steps 1 through 3.

TO PREPARE A DAY IN ADVANCE: Steps 1 through 3.

TO FREEZE: Best not frozen.

BEEF STROGANOFF

INGREDIENTS

1-1/2 lbs	tender steak (top sirloin)
	flour
	salt and pepper and seasoned salt
	butter or butter-oil combination
2	onions, chopped fine
1/2 lb	mushroom, sliced
1 clove	garlic, pressed
2 T	flour
2 T	melted butter
1 can	condensed consomme or bouillon
1 pint	sour cream
	salt, pepper, seasoned salt to taste
1 tsp	paprika
1 T	Worcestershire sauce
2 - 4 T	chopped parsley, optional
	paprika, optional

METHOD

1. Cut meat into thin strips, approximately 1" x 2" x 1/8 or 1/4". Dredge meat with flour which has been seasoned with salt and pepper and seasoned salt.

2. In a large skillet, melt approximately 4 T butter or butter-oil mixture over high heat. Saute the meat quickly — must be brown outside, underdone on the inside. Toss it or turn it as it browns. Don't crowd pan or most will stew and steam instead of browning. Oil must be hot to do this properly. Remove from pan and keep warm. (Add more butter or oil if necessary, as the meat browns.)

3. In 4 T butter, saute onions, mushrooms and garlic, until onions are golden yellow. Keep warm with meat.

4. Make cream sauce: Add 2 T flour to 2 T melted butter and cook a minute or so, until flour is blended and not raw. Add 1 can consomme or

bullion. Stir to thicken.

5. On low heat, stir in 1 pint sour cream to sauce and add salt, pepper, and seasoned salt to taste, 1 tsp paprika and 1 T Worcestershire sauce.

6. At serving time, heat sauce over low heat, add mushrooms, onions and beef. May garnish with chopped parsley and paprika for color.

TO PREPARE IN A.M.: Steps 1 through 5, be careful not to cook too much or sour cream may curdle and separate from sauce. Do not keep ingredients warm.

TO PREPARE A DAY IN ADVANCE: Steps 1 through 5, refrigerate beef, onions and mushrooms and sauce separately. Put together just before serving.

TO FREEZE: May freeze beef, onions and mushrooms together and sauce separately. Thaw. Heat sauce carefully on low heat and add meat mixture and heat through and serve. Optional: May leave out sour cream, and when reheating sauce, add sour cream them heat.

Note: This is a really delicious Stroganoff — not the overcooked kind that usually uses round steak — cooked this way, you can have a lovely Stroganoff, rare or medium rare.

Red Burgundy

BEEF BOURGUIGNON
(Serves 6 to 10)

INGREDIENTS

3 lbs	*stewing beef cut into 2" cubes*
	oil — olive and peanut preferred
1	*minced carrot*
2	*minced onions*
1 tsp	*salt*
1/4 tsp	*fresh ground pepper*
	flour
3 cups	*dry red wine (Burgundy or Chianti)*
2-3 cups	*beef stock or bouillon*
1 T	*tomato paste (optional)*
2 cloves	*mashed garlic*
1/2 tsp	*thyme*
1	*bay leaf*
2 lbs	*small pearl onions, sauteed*
1 lb	*fresh mushrooms, sauteed*
	seasoned salt to taste
	minced garlic

METHOD

1. Dry beef in paper towels. Set oven temperature to 325 degrees.

2. In 2 T oil, quickly saute minced carrot and onions. Remove.

3. In same pot, or in a large frying or saute pan, heat 2 T more oil. Mix 2 to 4 T flour with 1 tsp salt and 1/4 tsp ground pepper, and toss beef cubes in seasoned flour. (You may add some seasoned salt to the flour if you desire.) Saute the meat, a few pieces at a time, in the hot oil until it is browned all over. Remove the done pieces and repeat process until you have used all the meat.

4. Return all the meat to the pot or casserole, add the carrot and onions, and toss to mix.

5. Stir in the 3 cups wine, and enough stock to barely cover the meat. Add the tomato paste, garlic, 1/2 tsp thyme, 1 bay leaf, crumbled. Bring to a simmer on top of the stove.

6. Cover the casserole or pot and put in lower half of oven, simmer slowly for 3 to 4 hours, or until meat is done when it is tender and a fork pierces it easily.

7. While the beef is cooking, saute the onions and mushrooms separately and set aside.

8. When meat is tender, remove fat from the sauce. Taste for seasoning.

9. Add mushrooms and onions and decorate with minced parsley. Serve with noodles, rice or potatoes.

TO PREPARE IN A.M.: Steps 1 through 9, 20 minutes before serving, simmer covered, slowly until heated through.

TO PREPARE A DAY IN ADVANCE: Steps 1 through 9, 20 minutes before serving, simmer covered, slowly until heated through.

TO FREEZE: Steps 1 through 9, 20 minutes before serving, simmer covered, slowly until heated through.

Syrah

I've been told this tastes like Chasen's famous chili:

CHILI

INGREDIENTS

1/2 lb (1 cup)	red pinto beans dry
1 T	vinegar
1 lb	chopped green peppers
1-1/2 T	oil
1-1/2 lbs	chopped onion
2 cloves	garlic
1/2 cup	chopped parsley
3-1/2 lbs	ground beef or combination beef and pork (and ground turkey)
1/3 cup	chili powder
2 T	salt
1-1/2 tsp	cumin
1-1/2 tsp	M.S.G. (optional)
5 cups	solid pack tomatoes or crushed tomatoes

METHOD

1. Wash beans and soak overnight in water to cover, plus 1 T vinegar. Next day, simmer covered in water 1 hour, or till tender. Set aside.

2. Saute the green peppers in 11/2 T oil for 5 minutes and add chopped onions, 2 cloves garlic — put through a garlic press, and 1/2 cup chopped parsley. Use a 4 to 6 qt heavy bottom pot.

3. To the onion-pepper mixture, add the ground meat, and saute, using a large fork or wooden spoon to break up the meat. When meat is no longer red, stir in 1/3 cup chili powder, 2 T salt, 11/2 tsp pepper, 11/2 tsp cumin and if desired the 11/2 tsp M.S.G. Cook 10 minutes.

4. Add to the meat mixture 5 cups tomatoes. Simmer for 11/2 hours.

5. 20 minutes before serving, add beans (and liquid if desired), and serve in a large bowl accompanied with chopped fresh onions. If you prefer, you may serve the chili in one bowl and the beans in another, to be combined as desired.

TO PREPARE IN A.M.: Steps 2 through 4.

TO PREPARE A DAY IN ADVANCE: Step 1, and 2 through 4.

TO FREEZE: I find it saves room in the freezer to freeze the chili only (steps 2 through 4), although the whole thing with the beans added freezes beautifully.

TEX MEX DESSERT

Fry a flour tortilla in hot (375 degrees) peanut oil or oil and butter, pushing down at the center to make a bowl shape (or use special tostada forms). When lightly brown, remove. May sprinkle with cinnamon and sugar if desired. When ready to serve, put a scoop or two or three of ice cream in center (coffee flavor is nice) and pour Kahlua or other favorite liqueur over and serve immediately. I have truly never had this as good in any restaurant. It takes a bit of time, but well worth the effort.

Port

or

Cream Sherry

or

Late Harvest

Reisling

The fragrance from this red fruit soup is so wonderful you'll feel like putting a dab behind your ears:

SOUPE DE FRUIT ROUGE
(Serves 4)

INGREDIENTS

1 bottle	(750 ml to 1 liter) red wine (Bordeaux)
1/2	vanilla bean
1	cinnamon stick
1	clove
7 oz (200 gr)	sugar
1/2	orange
1/2	lemon
7 oz (200 gr)	strawberries
	mint leaves
7 oz (200 gr)	raspberries
3-1/2 oz (100 gr)	red currants (optional)

METHOD

1. Reduce the red wine, vanilla bean, cinnamon, clove, sugar until half remains.

2. Combine in a bowl, the half orange and lemon cut in round slices, the strawberries and some mint leaves. Remove wine from heat and cool 20 minutes and pour over fruit. Let sit 10 minutes, still a little warm.

3. Combine raspberries with some mint leaves and add to the cooled mixture. Refrigerate.

4. Serve chilled.

TO PREPARE IN A.M.: Steps 1 through 4.

TO PREPARE A DAY IN ADVANCE: Steps 1 through 4, but berries will be softer.

TO FREEZE: Steps 1 through 4, but berries will be softer.

Note: May use champagne or sauterne or dry white wine instead of Bordeaux. If using fresh currants, add in step 2, bottles or canned in step 3. Amount of sugar can vary depending on fruit. May use other fruits such as peaches, but then it won't be "rouge."

So nice with a glass of Cream Sherry or late Harvest Reisling:

MINA'S RUGGULACH

INGREDIENTS

1 cup	*cream cheese*
1/2 lb	*butter*
2 cups	*flour*
1 T	*vanilla*
	flour
	cinnamon
	ground nuts
	raisins (puffed in hot water)

METHOD

1. Mix cream cheese, butter, flour and vanilla in food processor or mixer until very well blended. Refrigerate overnight.

2. Divide dough into 4 parts. Sprinkle rolling surface with flour, cinnamon and sugar. Roll each quarter into a 10" circle. Mix more cinnamon and sugar and put under and over while rolling. When rolled out, sprinkle with cinnamon, sugar, nuts and raisins. Cut into 8 triangles, and roll up. Put tip down on baking sheet.

4. Bake 30 minutes at 350 degrees.

TO PREPARE IN A.M.: Steps 1 through 4.

TO PREPARE A DAY IN ADVANCE: Steps 1 through 4.

TO FREEZE: Steps 1 through 4.

This sweet omelette from Tuscany makes an unusual dessert, or is nice for breakfast or brunch:

FRITTATA CON LE PERE
(PEAR OMELETTE)
(Serves 1 or 2)

INGREDIENTS

3 T	flour
1/2 cup	milk
1 T	pear or orange liqueur (optional)
	or 1 T lemon juice
2	large eggs, beaten
1 heaping T	sugar
	grated rind of 1/2 orange
2	pears, peeled and grated or sliced
3 T	butter
	confectioners' sugar

METHOD

1. Mix the flour, milk, liqueur or lemon juice, eggs, sugar, and orange rind, beating well to make a light batter. Stir in the pears.

2. Heat the butter in an 8-inch (Teflon is best) frying pan and pour in the pear mixture, making sure the mixture is level in the pan. Cook until set and golden brown on the bottom. Either invert onto a plate, then slide back into pan, so that underdone side is on bottom of the fry pan, and finish cooking, or leave in pan and put under broiler without flipping and finish cooking the top.

3. When cooked, slide out onto a serving plate and sprinkle with confectioners' sugar.

Though its roots are in Lombardy, I first tasted this dessert at a restaurant in Los Angeles. It's so simple to put together, and the ingredients can be kept on hand. Served in crystal goblets, with crisp cookies, you have an elegant dessert. It could also be used to frost a cake.

CASTAGNE E CREMA
CHESTNUT DESSERT
(Serves 1 or 2)

INGREDIENTS

7-8 oz	sweetened chestnut puree (canned or homemade)
8 oz	heavy cream, whipped
4 T	rum or other liqueur

METHOD

1. Flavor the chestnut puree with 2 T rum. Whip the cream and flavor with 2 T rum. Swirl equal amounts of each together.

Note: The amount of rum can be reduced or left out if desired.

Translated, this means "English soup." Probably, an Italian visited England and was so taken with their Trifle Pudding, that he brought it back with a new name and a few variations. This is so easy to make if you use the instant pudding (and it's really just as good) and people will never know that you didn't slave away in the kitchen. It's best made a day or two ahead, but if you do, don't put the topping of whipped cream on until the day you are going to serve it.

ZUPPA INGLESE DE ROMA
(Serves 8)

INGREDIENTS

16-20 oz	*sponge or pound cake*
6 T	*rum*
6 T	*creme de cacao or Marsala wine*
2 cups	*crema pasticciera or instant vanilla pudding made with:*
2 cups	*cream or half and half.*
1-2 cups	*fresh fruit (peaches, raspberries, etc.)*
4 T	*Grand Marnier or orange liquor*
1 cup	*whipping cream*
1-2 T	*confectioners' sugar (powdered)*

METHOD

1. Cut the cake into thin layers and sprinkle half with rum (you may dilute with a little water if you wish) and half with creme de cacao.

2. Make crema pasticciera or vanilla pudding and cool. Sprinkle Grand Marnier over fruit, add to cooled pudding.

3. Whip cream and sweeten to taste with confectioners' sugar.

To Assemble: In a crystal bowl, or springform pan, put a layer of cake then a layer or pudding with fruit. Decorate cake with whipped cream. Refrigerate.

Vegetables & Starch

When I first began catering everyone wanted this recipe. Now all can have it.

PAULA'S BARLEY CASSEROLE

INGREDIENTS

2 T	butter or margarine
1 cup	barley
1	small minced onion
2 - 10 oz cans	chicken broth
1/2 tsp	marjoram
1/4 tsp	oregano
1/2 tsp	salt
1/4 tsp	pepper

METHOD

1. Melt 2 T butter, add 1 cup barley and onion. Cook till barley is slightly toasted.

2. Add remaining ingredients and cover tightly and simmer 35-40 minutes, or until liquid is absorbed, or bake 350 degrees for 1 hour.

TO PREPARE IN A.M.: Steps 1 and 2, and reheat, or step 1 and proceed with step 2 one hour before serving.

TO PREPARE A DAY IN ADVANCE: Steps 1 and 2, and reheat, or step 1 and proceed with step 2 one hour before serving.

TO FREEZE: Steps 1 and 2, defrost and reheat in double boiler.

GREEN BEANS ÉCHALOTE WITH BASIL
(Serves 6)

INGREDIENTS

20 oz	*frozen whole green beans (string) (or fresh cleaned)*
2 to 4 T	*butter (sweet preferred)*
1/4 cup	*minced shallots*
	salt and pepper to taste
1 T	*minced fresh basil*

METHOD

1. Thaw or clean beans.

2. In a wok or large frying pan, melt butter, add minced shallots and saute about 1 minute.

3. Add green beans and stir and toss until hot and coated with butter and shallots.

4. Add salt and pepper and minced basil and toss and stir another few seconds. Serve immediately.

TO PREPARE IN A.M.: Steps 1 and 2.

TO PREPARE A DAY IN ADVANCE: Step 1 and mince shallots or step 2.

TO FREEZE: No.

Note: If there are any leftovers, add some vinaigrette dressing and marinate overnight and use as a salad.

193

A very pretty vegetable that can be made well ahead of time.

TOMATO STUFFED WITH MUSHROOMS

INGREDIENTS
8	*firm ripe tomatoes*
1/4 lb	*butter*
11/4 lb	*cleaned, sliced mushrooms*
1 cup	*sour cream*
1 tsp	*flour*
1 T	*flour*
1/4 tsp	*fines herbes seasoning (Spice Island)*
1 tsp	*chopped parsley*
2 T	*dry sherry*
	salt
	pepper
	seasoned salt
	sesame seeds
	paprika

METHOD

1. Cut a slice from the top of the tomatoes and with a spoon carefully scoop out the soft part. Set the shells aside upside down to drain.

2. In a large skillet, melt 1/4 lb butter and saute the 11/4 lbs sliced mushrooms until all moisture evaporates.

3. Mix 1 cup sour cream with 1 T and 1 tsp flour and blend in with the mushrooms over low heat until thick and bubbly. Be careful not to boil as the sour cream could curdle. Stir in 1/4 tsp fines herbes, 1 tsp chopped parsley, 2 T dry sherry, salt, pepper and seasoned salt to taste. Cool.

4. Stuff the tomatoes loosely. Sprinkle the top with toasted sesame seeds and a light dusting of paprika. (May substitute ground blanched almonds for the sesame seeds if desired.)

5. Bake at 375 degrees for 15 minutes or until bubbly. Serve immediately.

TO PREPARE IN A.M.: Steps 1 through 4.

TO PREPARE A DAY IN ADVANCE: Steps 1 through 4.

TO FREEZE: Do not freeze.

Drinking, Aging and Storing Wine

Drinking wine involves many things, such as what glass or cup to drink from, how cold the wine should be, whether or not the wine should be poured from the bottle into another container. Some of the answers to these questions depend on the wine, the time, the setting, and who is doing the drinking. A delightful picnic wine might taste good from paper cups—and I've enjoyed some right from the bottle passed around. But most wine is probably purchased to drink with meals; so the following discussions are primarily directed toward drinking with dining.

STEMWARE

The term "stemware" refers to glassware used for drinking wine or, more specifically, the shape of the glass. There's a lot of esoterica on this subject, and in fancy restaurants they often have different shaped glasses for different wines. Clear glass is always preferable, so you can see the color of the wine. For practical purposes there are only two important pointers: don't drink wine out of small glasses, and don't fill up the glass too full. Let's talk about each of these two points:

As I mentioned above, as much as 80% of the taste of wine is based on smell. In order to get much aroma out of mild smelling substances the molecules to be smelled have to be collected together in some space. It's hard to smell something if you're standing outside in a high wind: the molecules don't collect, and are quickly spread away by the wind. So the ideal conditions for smelling, and therefore tasting, are to have a space where the molecules can collect, and into which you can put your nose so as to draw these molecules into your smell system.

An adequately large glass bowl, filled less than half full with wine, is ideal for that purpose. If the glass is too small or too full, there isn't enough space for the molecules to collect in, nor for you to put your nose into.

For financial reasons, many bars and restaurants serve wine by the glass in small, 4 oz. glasses. They do that because customers complain if they serve a glass less than half full. The customers would rather have 4 oz. of wine in a 4 oz. glass, than 4 oz. of wine in an 8 oz. glass. Then too, to finish the first bottle of wine and sell a second bottle before the end of the meal, the waiter keeps pouring wine into everybody's glasses to "top them off."

It would be hard to break these habits, since finances usually take precedence over esthetics, but you can try. Ask for a larger glass. Ask the waiter or wine steward not to fill the glass more than half full. And of course, at home you can have the right kind of glasses and pour small amounts into them. Save those small glasses for sweet Port or Sherry wines, which, when served after dinner, have enough strong flavor and sweetness on the tongue that they do not require an accumulation of molecules for the nose and tastebuds to react.

TEMPERATURE AND BREATHING

Temperature, of course, has to do with the question whether or not a wine should be chilled when served, and if so how much. Breathing deals with the controversial issue of whether wine should be allowed to come into contact with air (oxygen) for some period of time before drinking it.

In the United States, white wine is kept in the refrigerator, then served in an iced bucket, so that it is just above freezing temperature. Red wine is left sitting on a shelf, sometimes above the stove, shaken up a bit while brought to the table and the cork fight ensues, then quickly served at room temperature. We're lucky if we can get the waiter to open it in time for the first course.

But traditionally red and white wine came from the "cave," where it was about 56 degrees Fahrenheit, and the white wine served at once; the red wine, depending on the type, was brought out one or two hours before the meal, opened, and allowed to sit until mealtime. Even now, when I am buying wines at farmhouses in France and Italy, and they invite me to lunch, I note that their red wine has been poured into a carafe, and been sitting for a while before mealtime.

Here are the conclusions I have drawn from these experiences.

First of all, wine does taste different when it is chilled, particularly when over-chilled. For me, when white wine is really cold I can't taste much of the wine flavor. The flavors come out more fully when the wine is roughly at room temperature. But still I prefer most white wine slightly chilled, because flavor isn't everything—temperature itself is one aspect of pleasure in drinking wine. So when I have wine in a restaurant, after it is slightly chilled I ask the waiter to take it out of the ice bucket for a while so that it stays just slightly chilled, and not too cold.

Most red wine also tastes better to me slightly chilled. Beaujolais wines are usually served chilled. Remember, most wines are not fine old wines to be aged, but young, regional wines made to be drunk while young. These wines, like Beaujolais, for me go better with food when slightly chilled—about the temperature of a wine cellar, 55-60 degrees Fahrenheit.

But I prefer some rather special red wines to be decanted (the fancy word for pouring the wine out of the bottle into a decanter—a special glass bottle for holding wine) and then aired until they reach room temperature. This is a very controversial subject in the United States (less so in Europe). No scientific study that I've seen confirms that "oxygenating" wine improves its taste. But research on taste is very primitive. To paraphrase what the U.S. Supreme court wrote about pornography: I can't define it, but I know it when I see it. So I can't prove that some wines taste better when oxygenated, but I know its true for my taste buds.

Which wines benefit from aeration? Again, this is a tough question to answer. In general, I would say full bodied tannic red wines with some years remaining before they start to lose body; a new Barolo, for example, just bottled will benefit from aeration. We would expect the wine to continue improving in the bottle for at least 6 more years, and maybe 10 to 20. This wine will smooth out, and some of the tannins mellow, if decanted and left out for 2-3 hours until it reaches room temperature, before it is drunk. By the way, just taking out the cork, as some restaurants do, doesn't aerate the wine. It just aerates the small surface area at the top of the bottle. To air out the wine you either have to pour it into another container, or into the glasses.

Whether older wines that have reached their prime should also be decanted and left to air is an even more controversial subject. First of all, what do we mean by "older." Generally speaking, wine is young for 2-3 years after it is bottled. Not all wine holds up this long, but most do. Fine red wines made for long aging can be called "young" after six years or more, because they are not nearly ready to drink. So "old" and "young" are relative terms, depending on the aging potential of the wine.

Certainly there are times when a bottle of well aged wine is opened and poured, and tastes good for a few minutes, then goes somewhat flat. To have aerated that bottle would have killed it before it was tasted. So in general I would avoid decanting or airing an older bottle, unless you know from a previous bottle that it gets better after the second or third glass.

There is another reason that wine is decanted, other than to oxygenate it: as some red wines age, acids and tannins fall out of the liquid solution to the bottom of the bottle. This residue, called sediment, if mixed into the liquid wine makes it visually unpleasant, and the sediment can adversely affect the taste and texture of the wine.

For this reason, in many fine restaurants fine, older red wine is poured from the original bottle into a new glass bottle. The original bottle is usually left on the table, so that you can continue to admire the label if you drink so much that you forget what you are drinking. Sometimes decanting is done very ceremoniously, with special equipment. A candle is placed under the bottle to light up the liquid (to better see the sediment) as was done in the old days in the dark wine cellars, and the wine is slowly poured through a silver funnel until just before the sediment begins to flow.

There are some wines that benefit from decanting, because they have so much sediment in them that it's impossible to keep it from the glass. But by and large decanting for this reason is a sham. The bigger problem is that when the wine steward brings the wine to the table he is shaking it, and moving the sediment around in the bottle. Then when he (or she, many restaurants have the waiters or waitresses open the bottles) takes the cork out of the bottle he or she again shakes the bottle around. Whatever little sediment there was in the bottle (which easily could have been kept in the bottom of the bottle and controlled by careful pouring) is now mixed throughout the wine. So decanting won't help anyway.

The fact is that wine bottles, especially the Bordeaux shaped bottle, are designed to keep the sediment in the "shoulder" of the bottle as the wine is poured, and, if the wine is not shaken up and is poured carefully (and not to the last drop) the sediment will stay in the bottle.

There is probably little you can do about these problems in restaurants, but at home you can handle the wine carefully and avoid the need to decant except for young tannic red wines that need it, or that special old bottle that has a lot of sediment in it. For that special bottle, just let it sit still overnight before you decant it.

AGING AND STORAGE

I've mentioned several times that most wine is better when drunk young, in the first one or two years after it is bottled. I've also mentioned how sad it is that so much of the small production that will improve in the bottle is drunk well before it has reached its prime. Now let's talk a bit about when and how you may want to let certain wines age.

There is no question that those who drank up their 1985 premier cru Bordeaux before 1990, or their 1990 Barolo's before 1995, lost a chance to enjoy something special by keeping those wines another 5-10 years or more before drinking them. But these were special years for those wines, and much of what we know about these wines came from drinking them during this period, and seeing that they had these special characteristics that would allow them to continue to improve with age.

For most wines, even the fine ones we expect to age well, it's really hard to tell how long they will continue to improve. And, to most tastes, its better to drink the wine when too young than when too old (although some people, including me, like wines just past their prime). The bottom line is that unless you are extremely knowledgeable about the wine, if you are going to allow it to age in your cellar it is preferable to have several bottles (or a case) and drink a bottle every one or two years, and make notes, to keep track of the progress.

This may not be as painful as its sounds. While there is a lot of hoopla about wonderful aged wines—with much justification—most wine is plenty good well before its prime. The main thing to avoid is drinking really big wines when very young. I remember tasting a late harvest Zinfandel when it was four years old, and it was terrible. Only after about 15 years in the bottle did it become drinkable, and then, after 20 years in the bottle, it was wonderful. I've had similar experiences with Bordeaux and Barolo on a lesser time scale—drinking them one or two years after bottling, and finding them too tannic and without much flavor, then finding great improvement after 4-5 years.

As wine ages, it changes. Take Bordeaux as an example. As really well made Bordeaux ages the color fades from deep red with a purple tint, to a more red brick color, particularly around the edges. When young the taste is of cherries and plums and dark berries, with some herbs, wood and oak. As the wine ages these tastes subside, and evolve into a more complex flavor of spicy berries with scents of tobacco and dried fruits. The tannins lessen, making for a more mellow feel in the mouth, and the aftertaste deepens.

If you want to put aside some wines to age, there are several ways to do it. Wine should be kept with the bottles on their sides so that the corks remain moist, in a dark room where light cannot affect the wine. The two biggest enemies to proper wine storage are movement, and change in temperature. The bottles should remain still, at a steady temperature. Change in temperature causes the corks to swell or shrink, and this is why you should examine a bottle served in a restaurant before it is opened, so that you can see if the cork is intact.

Many homes have an area in the back of a closet on the ground floor that is relatively cool, gets no sun or heat, and is adequate to age wines. Wines aged at room temperature, however, will age more quickly than those kept at the ideal temperature of 55 to 60 degrees Fahrenheit. The slower aging process is preferable. Wine lockers that keep wines at the preferred temperature are available for rent at very reasonable rates in many wine stores. Or you can buy any one of a number of different wine storage cabinets made for the home that are cooled electrically. These come in different sizes, styles and qualities. There are also companies that fit a home closet or basement with a cooling unit, to make a professional-like storage area.

Only through reading about the wines, and from personal experience with aged wines, will you come to fully appreciate properly aged wines.

Wine and Health

In the United States there are many people who harbor an innate distrust of alcohol, which is why it is so heavily regulated. Maybe this is because alcohol was heavily abused during the early part of our history. Then too, the fact that we have become a society so dominated by the automobile, and the fact that alcohol does increase the risk of error in driving, has given legitimacy to concerns over the improper use of alcohol.

As a result of this distrust, and these concerns, drinking in general, including moderate servings of wine with dinner, is frowned upon by many people in our society. But, as a result of recent medical research, these attitudes may be changing, and we may be at the beginning of an accelerating upswing in the number of people who drink wine in moderation.

It's pretty clear now that regular, moderate consumption of alcohol is associated with a "very low risk of death from coronary heart disease," and that "people who drink alcohol regularly tend to have higher blood levels of protective h.d.l.'s, or high-density lipoproteins, which carry cholesterol out of the body and presumably help to keep coronary arteries unclogged. Red wine, by far the most popular alcoholic beverage in France, is believed to be the most beneficial since, in addition to the effects of the alcohol on h.d.l., substances in red grapes appear to inhibit the formation of blood clots."

—*New York Times Health section, Dec. 28, 1994*
reporting on a study at U. of Calif., San Diego.

This report on the beneficial effects of red wine was confirmed by research at both Harvard University and California State University, Fresno. The essence of these studies suggests that red wine contains the same helpful chemical that is in aspirin, and therefore a glass of wine each day is similar to an aspirin a day, which is now recommended by many physicians.

Another study recently reported in Wine Spectator magazine, is based on a report in the British Medical Journal. According to that report, a 12-year study in Copenhagen indicated a 49 percent reduction in mortality from vascular and cerebrovascular diseases in people who drank three to five glasses of wine per day.

Morten Gronbaek, from the Institute of Preventive Medicine at Copenhagen Municipal Hospital, was one of the authors of the study.

206

He believes that antioxidants and flavonoids, which some medical authorities believe prevent coronary heart disease, may be present in red wines.

The danger in assuming that wine is good for health has to do with the human tendency to over-consume. What's not yet clear is how many people can drink one or two glasses of wine a day, and not proceed to six or eight or more. It's no good to prevent heart disease if you're going to die from cirrhosis of the liver or a head-on automobile accident.

There are other problems with drinking wine. If you are diabetic, for example, the alcohol, which converts to sugar in the body, will almost certainly throw off your insulin regulation. People prone to depression may become depressed with moderate consumption of alcohol. And people with a tendency to be overweight may find that the consumption of alcohol adds to their weight problem. Combining alcohol with certain medications can be a serious error, so if you are taking any medication it only makes sense to check with a doctor before taking a drink. In general, however, doctors with whom I've consulted tell me that alcohol is not a problem in combination with antibiotics.

As anyone who has ever read a wine label knows, wine contains sulfites. Some people are allergic to sulfites. My doctor tells me that many foods contain sulfites in much larger quantities than a bottle of wine, and that some government agency should be requiring that label on foods as well. If you find that wine gives you a headache, or makes you sick, it might be the sulfites. You might want to go to a doctor and be sure, because if you are allergic to sulfites you should avoid them in foods as well as wine. Many people who think they are allergic to the sulfites in wine are allergic to something else, and find that they can drink some wines and not others—for example, dry wines, but not sweet wines.

For most people, wine adds pleasure to life. As is so often the case, excess is the enemy. It's important to know yourself, and monitor what you are doing.

SO WHY ALL THIS FUSS ABOUT WINE?

Pleasure is an important part of life for most of us. There are some pleasures that are immediate, such as eating, drinking, and sex. Some pleasures are immediate in part, but are experienced over a long period of time as they vary in degree, like a warm friendship, or watching a child grow into adulthood. And some pleasures are more cerebral, such as those Proust describes in his novels, as he remembers pleasures from the past.

For those who enjoy wine, the wine becomes a messenger of all these pleasures, and more. There is the immediate pleasure of the taste, and the enhanced pleasure of the accompanying food. There are the pleasures that arise from sharing wine with friends, discussing it, using it as a reason to get together. And the nature of the taste experience, connected as it is to the brain, is ideally suited to act as a reminder of past experiences with wine, past extraordinary meals, special bottles, and special events.

There are two additional pleasures connected with wine.

Through our long cultural history wine has taken on a ceremonial aspect. For many it is used in religious ceremonies, used to christen our ships as they slide into the sea for the first time, used to wish our loved ones well as they marry or celebrate other special occasions.

Finally, throughout our long cultural history, almost every culture exhibits keen interest in mind-altering drugs, including alcoholic beverages. Trances are still an important part of many religious ceremonies among diverse groups in many areas of the world. Going into a trance today in the more civilized parts of the world is frowned upon, and might get you committed to an institution. But the subtle trance-like effects of alcoholic beverages remain socially acceptable, and, I believe, act as an outlet for this apparently normal craving men and women have for this type of experience.

There are precious few such sources of such diversity of pleasure available to us at $10 per bottle!

ArticlesFrom The Palisadian Post

WINE AND TURKEYS

I have a friend who says that every holiday season he feels like the turkey, because he doesn't know what wine to serve with the holiday meals.

Because Californians are so used to drinking Chardonnay, that's the wine typically matched with roast turkey. Sometimes I read a recommendation for a Riesling, the delicious white wine of Germany with a distinctive flavor; and sometimes I see an adventurous writer suggest Beaujolais, the light, fruity wine from the area just south of Burgundy. Certainly these are good suggestions, and will please many palates.

But in the south of France, and in many hillside communities in Italy, we are more likely to see, next to the roast turkey or other poultry dishes, a bottle of rosé. Rosé is essentially a light red wine. It is made from the same red grapes that are used in red wine, and, in fact, can be made from just about any of the varieties used to make red wine. The difference is that the grapes are kept in contact with the juice for less time when the winemaker wants to produce rosé. And the style of winemaking used is often different from that used to make red wine, so that the winemaker can create a wine that is fresher, less tannic, and ready to drink at an earlier age.

There is as much or more diversification in the production of rose wines than in red or white wines. Dry, medium, and sweet wines are made, as well as light, full bodied, and fruity ones. Some of us are old enough to remember the craze in the United States for Lancers, a sparkling rose made in Portugal and sold in little ceramic bottles. And throughout California these days, one finds white zinfandel everywhere-a sweet rosé that is better as an aperitif than an accompaniment to food.

There are a number of rosé wines made in California, but most are boutique wines of small production. The most popular imported rosés are from three areas of France: rosé d'Anjou, from the Loire valley (near Gerard Depardieu's vineyards), rosés from the Rhone valley, near the town of Avignon, and the many rosé wines from Provence, in the South.

Rosé d'Anjou is a beautiful orange color, with a mild nose and a hint of sweetness. Rosés from the Rhone valley are typically more dry, and slightly heavier-a bit more like red wine. The Rhone rosés are redder in color, and somewhat more full flavored. To my palate they are perfect with roasted poultry. As with other wines of the Rhone valley, the better wines carry the name of the town where they are produced, such as Lirac The wines from the Provence region of France, where more rosé is consumed each year than any other region, vary greatly in color, taste and price. Certainly one of the most popular both there and here is the rosé of Chateau Minuty, a vineyard just outside of San Tropez.

This year when you toast your family and friends over the holiday dinner, look through a glass of rosé and start the year by looking at the world through rose-colored wine.

WINE LISTS

In our little corner of Los Angeles we are fortunate to have tremendous diversity of restaurants and wine lists. Valentino Restaurant, in Santa Monica, is recognized as having one of the best wine cellars in the world! Within a 15 minute ride we can find ethnic cuisine, with matching wines, from a dozen cultures. At Michael's you can order wine grown by the owner himself right in Malibu. Perhaps best of all, we have a number of small, family run restaurants, reminiscent of small towns in France and Italy, whose owners have carefully selected special wines to match the menu. In the next few articles in this column we will visit some of those restaurants together, reviewing their wine lists.

Before launching into such a review, however, let me to explain what I look for on the wine list when I go to a restaurant. Simply put, I look for selection, diversity, vintage and price.

Selection refers to the kind of wines on the list. A list with only medium quality, commonly known wines, is not very interesting. This error is most often seen in chain restaurants that have accepted some wine distributor's "standard" pre-printed wine list. These lists typically have one merlot, one cabernet, one or two chardonnays, and one white zinfandel. Such a list is about as interesting as reading a telephone book.

Diversity includes a number of elements: geography, region, type, and type of grape. A really interesting wine list includes wines from both California and Europe. It may also include some wines from other areas such as Australia, New Zealand, South Africa, Germany, Oregon, Washington, Chile, and so forth. Some of these countries, especially France and Italy, have great diversity of wines from different regions.

The type of wine and the grape concerns the flavor to be expected from the wine. Type can be broken down into various categories, such as sweet vs. dry, red vs. white, strong vs. mild flavor, and high or low acid. The grape means the primary grape from which the wine is made: cabernet, pinot noir, zinfandel, chardonnay, etc. An interesting wine list should include wines with a variety of flavors, so the guest can match the flavor with his or her mood and food selection.

Vintage means the year of harvest. A wine list that omits the vintage is suspect. Careless waiters sometimes bring a wine from a different year than the one on the list. It is surprising how often the one on hand is not as good as the one on the list, but no adjustment in price is made. Vintage is especially important on the wine lists of fine dining restaurants. There's a world of difference in taste and value between certain wines of great vintage years, and the same wine by the same producer in a poor year, and it does not feel good to pay a premium price for a fine wine with a famous name and be disappointed in the taste because it's from a poor vintage not reflected in the price.

Finally we come to price. This warrants a column in itself, which I hope to write in a few months. Wine pricing in many restaurants is a disgrace, and inhibits diners from enjoying a fine wine with dinner. I see wines that I can buy at a restaurant in France for $5 priced at $30 on some Los Angeles restaurant lists. Some restaurants have a rule of thumb that they mark up wines three times their cost-without regard to the quality, availability, or price level of the wine. But it isn't just raw cost I look at: a good list should include a few inexpensive wines, some medium priced wines, and a few expensive wines for special occasions. Fortunately, many restaurants in our area are run by sophisticated, knowledgeable people who are interested in offering their guests interesting wines at attractive prices. As you'll see in my next column, there are in fact some extraordinary values on the wine lists of some of our local restaurants.

A TOAST TO MAINLAND CHINA

Since second son Spencer can read and write both ancient and modern Chinese (he teaches Japanese literature, some of which from ancient times, to our never-ending surprise, turns out to be written in Chinese), we decided to reward his success in passing the exams needed for his Ph.D. with a trip together to China. Naturally, while there, we were interested in the local wine production.

As in most countries, wine is made everywhere, but there is one region particularly known for the production of fine wine, some of which is exported. In China it seems that there are two companies making "western style" wine, Great Wall, and Dynasty. Each makes a red wine called Cabernet, presumably made from the cabernet sauvignon grape, but I'm pretty sure some of the bottles I drank were from a gamay grape. The quality was mediocre, but the price was right (for western pockets-very expensive for locals). The white wines were better, and went well with much of the spicy food from the Sichuan and Hunan regions.

Genuine snake wine in Beijing Department Store

But it was pretty clear that the locals were drinking something else, so we decided to check it out. Our first opportunity was in a department store in Beijing. We were browsing through the food department when we spotted a selection of wines. The featured wine really captured out attention: on the counter were two large bottles filled with an amber liquid-each with a good-sized snake curled up inside.

Discussions with the saleslady disclosed, with a giggle, that snake essence was good for male virility. Accordingly, a snake is placed live in the bottle, then a highly alcoholic wine mixture is poured over it, drowning the snake for a higher purpose, and then the mixture is left to age for a few months.

The next week we were on a boat trip down the Yangtze River for a few days. Our bunks were approximately 14 inches in width, and the mattress was probably made of mahogany. This clearly impaired my ability to sleep through the night, and certainly did not improve my virility: even when my wife and I were at our thinnest we could not have shared one of these bunks. So, the next afternoon when a boat stewardess offered us a glass of snake wine, I gratefully accepted. And it was good. It was very alcoholic, and not floral, but it was mellow and flavorful. I didn't taste the snake at all.

A few days later we were in Shanghai, walking through a night market-restaurant district when we came upon a snake wine vendor. There were a number of snakes curled up in cages, with price tags on each cage, and there were barrels of dark, amber colored wine. I presume it was a "do-it-yourself" type snake-wine store, and I imagine it was quite delicious. Following my doctor's orders, however, I didn't eat or drink anything from a street vendor, so I missed out.

Looking back at our experiences in China reinforces what I always say about wine: the variety of experiences available with wine, its universality, and the interesting intercultural differences of wine are one of the reasons that an interest in wine makes life more interesting.

CRUISING IN BURGUNDY
May 1999

We're cruising through the heart of Burgundy on a 100-foot floating hotel with two friends from the Palisades. I think we picked the right friends to share the trip. Jill is an excellent cook, and she and Bonnie gather local products from the small towns along the way, and prepare them for our lunches on the boat. Today the local butcher recommends pigs ears in jelly, and "parsleyed ham grandmother's style." Harvey is interested in great restaurants, so he is in charge of locating and making reservations in some of the great restaurants along the way. I buy and serve the wines.

Harvey carefully prepared the trip well in advance, with lunch and dinner reservations at great restaurants along the way. While the booking agent balked at him talking with the boat captain in advance, we weren't worried about being able to communicate with him and his wife, since between Jill and myself we speak virtually all of the Western European languages fluently. Except Swisserdeutch. We both speak German, but neither of us understand hardly any of the German-Swiss language that has evolved into a separate linguistic category, so communication with the crew is limited to a few shared words of English, German, and French.

In addition, we've had to cancel most of the restaurant reservations, since the Saonne river is flooded and we had to divert up a canal so the boat can retain steerage. So much for careful planning in advance.

But France is incredibly beautiful, and along side of the boat are green pastures, forests and vineyards, with white cows and new-born colts. The small towns are pristine, and the people extremely friendly. We haven't seen one beer can, plastic bottle, or even piece of paper on the side of the canal or even along the roadways. There is virtually NO trash outside of a trash can, and even then it's carefully wrapped in plastic bags before it is put into the can. It's cleaner than Singapore!

Yesterday we stopped in Santenay, a city famous for its red Pinot Noir wines. I'd heard of a producer named Belland that makes famous wines here. When we arrived I discovered that there are six producers with Belland as their last name, all related, making wine here. But a little discussion with the local bartender led me to Roger Belland, the one I had in mind, even though the question was "very delicate" to answer, according to my friend the bartender.

M. Belland was a bit short when we arrived on his doorstep, and quickly explained that he had no wine left to sell. He was completely sold out, to the last bottle and didn't even have any for his own family to drink, thanks for stopping by come again next year. But after a bit of discussion about California, and children, he invited the four of us into his cave to taste barrel samples of the 1998 wines that would be bottled between September and November of this year.

The cellar was extensive and covered two levels underground. The barrel samples were wonderful, and we learned a lot about how the wines would be mixed from new oak barrels and older barrels, and the production techniques in general. There were significant differences between the six different wines we tasted. We agreed that M. Belland would send me a case of samples when they were bottled so I could place an order. We asked if he could direct us to any store in the area that might have a few of his bottles left for sale, but he assured me that all of his production had been purchased or exported by now.

That night we ate in the local upscale restaurant (Lobster Gazpacho and coq au vin), and in discussions with the hostess I discovered she had a bottle of M. Belland's 1993 Santenay in her cellar. Rarely have we enjoyed a wine more. Both because of its quality, and from the pleasure of having succeeded in having found a bottle to drink.

217

MORE CRUISING IN BURGUNDY

We're cruising on a canal boat through miles and miles of vineyards, most of which is of pinot noir vines. The pinot noir grape is the one from which most red Burgundy wine is made, and is considered one of the most difficult grapes to grow. A significant amount of pinot noir is now grown in California and Oregon, but most of the wines produced from these vines tastes quite different to me than the wines of Burgundy. The French say that it's because the soil and climate is different.

One thing is for sure: when you do find a really great red burgundy wine, it's an exception treat and an experience that will be remembered. Finding such a wine, however, is another story.

One thing we've learned from cruising in Burgundy is how much we don't know about the wine of Burgundy. I've been drinking Burgundy wine for about 30 years, and I recognize a lot of the names, such as Pommard (reputed to have been John Kennedy's favorite wine), Gevry-Chambertin, Vogne-Romanee, etc. But that information turns out to be meaningless in selecting a Burgundy wine. We've had Vogne-Romanee from the local market at $12 a bottle. Good, but not great. Other bottles with the same name on the label, from different vintages and from different producers, are selling out at $100 per bottle.

So we've started to keeps notes. One night we had a 1990 Gevry-Chambertin from Faviley for $65 in a restaurant, which was spectacular. Mild, with the nose of a flower garden, mouth filling and flavorful, with a slight sweetness on the aftertaste. The next night we had a 1995 Gevry-Chambertin from a producer I didn't recognize, for about the same price. It was full-bodied, and pleasant with dinner, but not nearly as exceptional.

We tried the same comparison with Pommard. One night we had a 1992 from a shipper whose name we recognized, which was $80 in a "Michelin star" restaurant. It was excellent. The following night we had a 1993 Pommard in another fine restaurant, slightly less expensive, but not nearly as flavorful, and totally lacking in the characteristic Pinot Noir flavors.

And so our experiments and education continue. Our conclusions so far are that to be a knowledgeable consumer of Burgundy wine requires a lot of detailed, precise knowledge of the vintage years and individual producers. For most consumers this is not practical. And given the prices of Burgundy wines, which are in very short supply compared to demand, most buyers will have to rely on knowledgeable wine salespeople or restaurant cellar masters.

THE BEST RESTAURANT IN THE WORLD

We just made our once-every-ten-years pilgrimage to our favorite restaurant in the world, Paul Bocuse, near Lyon, France. I first went there in the 1950's. Bonnie and I went there in 1962. In 1970 we went there again, but Bonnie was sick and only ordered tea. Chef Bocuse came out of the kitchen to commiserate with her, and was very solicitous. To make up for the small order, I ordered the famous truffle soup (with bits of foie gras in it) and the "Loup en croute." I figured if it was good enough for the dinner served to the President of France, it should be good enough for me.

We were there once in the 1980's, and again with our friends Harvey and Jill in 1999. By 1980 the restaurant had been redecorated, a new, beautiful room added, and the building painted a distinctive pastel color. In this decade we got an early start, by going in October of 2000.

In 1970, since Bonnie wasn't drinking (she doesn't drink white wine), I asked the Sommelier to bring me a half-bottle of his favorite Chablis. I still remember the taste-it was by far the best Chablis I had ever tasted. It had the distinctive taste of the Chardonnay grape, without oak, the tingle of acid on the tongue, and a long aftertaste with a trace of the chalky texture of the soil in that region.

In 1999, remembering my success in 1970, I again asked the sommelier for his recommendation for a red wine of the region. First he asked me a few questions to determine my taste in wines. Did I like a strong, full-bodied wine, or would I prefer something a bit lighter? Something very fruity, or more complex? And so forth. Then he produced a 1997 Saint-Joseph, "cuvee Prestige L'Amarybelle" made by Yves Cuilleron, in the town of Chavanay. Even though I had been on a tasting of Rhone wines for about a week, it was one of the most delicious Rhone's I'd had, then or since then. Furthermore, it was not expensive-especially for such a fine restaurant-at $40 for the bottle.

So this year I again put myself in the hands of the sommelier. Again he asked a few questions first. He suggested a Cote Rotie. I asked what he thought about wines with 5% white grape juice added, like Côte Rotie, mostly to show off how much I know about wines. He smiled, and explained to me that although that used to be the case years ago, now producers of Côte Rotie only put in about 1% Viognier, just enough to develop some perfume in the nose, and not enough to affect the taste. He was glad that I asked about it. So we settled on a 1998 Côte Rotie from Domain de Bonserine, from the town of Ampuis. Again it was very reasonably priced, on the low end of the wines on the list. It was good, but-to my taste-not great. The meal, on the other hand, was great, and the service perfect. Above all, it feels really good to be able to trust a knowledgeable sommelier in a really fine restaurant with a huge wine list. And it's always nice that Chef Bocuse is at the entrance of the restaurant to greet you when you arrive, stops by the table during lunch to check up on things, and again at the door to say goodbye. That's what I call "hands on" management.

According to the New York Times, the best Rhone wine list in the world is at the Le Restaurant a Beaugraviere, in Mondragon France, just south of Lyon (tel 04.90.40.82.54). I haven't been there yet, but it's going to be tough to compete with Paul Bocuse.

Chef Bocuse with the author

PROST!

We're cruising down the Elbe river just south of Berlin to Prague. Our boat looks like a floating football field, and the engines are so far behind us we haven't heard them yet. We expected the same mediocre food and wines on board as we had in Berlin, where we spent two weeks taking a German language refresher course. Our daughter, an immigration lawyer, suddenly has an influx of German and Russian clients, and claimed she needed it and we should join her, so we did. We're now working our way slowly to Italy and France, via Prague, to visit our usual vineyards.

Berlin was more exciting than we expected, but it is also a giant construction zone. The level of culture is very high, with numerous symphony orchestras and opera companies that we were lucky enough to enjoy. The beer was excellent and varied. The food and wine were another story.

My first hint about German wine came from several German friends that we visited on the way to Berlin. I noticed that both at home and at dinner in restaurants they were ordering French, Italian, and Spanish wines. I tentatively broached the subject by asking about German red wines. I got similar answers from both Gerhard, a dentist, and Jan, the CEO of a construction company: "yes, there is some red wine made in Germany." Then change of subject.

Necessity being the mother of invention, I mentioned that I was eager to try some of the famous German Rieslings and other white wines. This time I got another answer: "well, you really should go to the Moselle area if you want to try local German wines."

So I went to a local wine store in Berlin. As you can see from the picture, it didn't look like any wine store I've ever seen in the states. There were bottles of wine in shelves, but most of the customer action centered around various glass flasks on multi-tiered tables in the center of the store. One level turned out to be wines that were available by the glass, and a number of satisfied customers were sitting around, like at Starbucks, reading the paper and occasionally filling up a glass from the flasks. The other flasks contained various flavored oils and vinegars. I tried a couple of glasses of dry Riesling. There was none of the famous sweet Riesling available by the glass because, according to the clerk, "German people like dry wine." This was confirmed to me by a nice gentleman sitting at one of the tables, who-mainly with hand signals, said that sweet wine gave him a headache.

My real chance to focus on wine came on the boat. After the first dinner I asked what famous French chef was on duty: the food was spectacular. I was then introduced to a 20-year-old German boy in a chef's toque, who spoke perfect English, and turned out to be the chef. For one full week I was dazzled by the food, and it was a good opportunity to taste a variety of wines. From the substantial list of red wines available, only two were from Germany. The one we ordered one night, the Verrnberger Lindelberg 1998, was light in color-almost like Rosé-and tasted of the Pinot Noir grape, as in Burgundy. It went well with the smoked eel, which was rich and oily, and the roast lamb, that was lean and gamy. The waitress was surprised when I asked her to chill the red wine, but because of its lightness it was best served like a Beaujolais.

We had plenty of chances to sample the local white wines. On board I drank the 1998 Muller-Thurgau from Sachsen, and the Nieder-Florsheimer table wine. One evening the boat crew arranged a wine tasting in a local wine cellar during a stopover in Meissen. The 500 year old cellar was run by an attractive young women in

German peasant clothing who was way too serious about explaining the wines for the Americans on board, who wanted to drink more, and hear less. So I moved over to a table of four German men from Frankfort, who were having a 20 year fraternity reunion, so they could help me translate what the hostess was saying. During our hour together these gentlemen drank about one bottle each of the various local wines, so I know they enjoyed them. One of the reasons they came to Saxony, one said, was for the local wines.

The tasting consisted of five local wines. One was a blend of red and white wine. Two were from the Muller-Thurgau grape, a genetic combination, and the other two were also combinations of the Riesling grape with another variety. Two were very light in flavor, with no nose at all. The last three had a very floral nose, a clean citrus taste, and high acid. All of the wines had about a 20% lower alcohol level than traditional French and American wines. All the wines were for sale at about $4-5 per bottle.

So, Mervyn Hecht, famous wine writer for a prestigious California newspaper, traveled through Germany without ever drinking any of the famous Riesling wines from the Rhine valley. Oh well, the wines I did drink are in my memory, connected to my experiences from the trip. And that's really what wine is about for me.

Berlin wine tasting bar

BAD WORDS

Last Month I took my son-in-law Lars and grandson Erik hiking on Santa Cruz Island. Lars, an avid birder, was in search of the elusive and timid Santa Cruz Blue Scrub Jay, which lives only on that island. Erik was more impressed by the old, rusty tractors around the deserted farmhouse near the landing.

On the hike into the hills Erik asked me if I know any bad words. So I asked him if he knew any. He admitted that he did know one, and, when pressed to disclose it, admitted that his bad word was "stupid." At his request, I taught him a couple of new bad words, the word for "stupid" in Japanese, and the equivalent of "damn" in French. He seemed pleased with this, and repeated the words several times. Later, I heard him confide to his dad, "Grandpa doesn't know the "F" word."

In the wine business, the "F" word is Fruit. But, like Grandpa, not many wine writers seem to know it. When I read wine reviews, I read about "impressive" wines, with "structure" and "integrity." I read about wines that convey the taste of the terrain, an earthiness reminiscent of truffles and tobacco, a hint of chocolate, grassiness, tar, and heaven knows what else.

Those are not the tastes that I want to know about when deciding whether or not to drink a wine.

First of all I want to know if the wine has adequate fruit on the palate. If the grower was primarily interested in the quantity to be produced, the grapes will not produce a wine with an intense fruit flavor. But if the grower trimmed the vines, the grapes will produce an intense fruit flavor.

Next I want to know the residual sugar. Both red and white wines can be very dry, very sweet, or somewhere in-between. With some foods, like oysters, I like a very dry white wine. With Chinese food I prefer a white wine with a touch of sweetness. And with fruit for dessert, I like a sweet white wine. Some red wines are OK if very dry, but a touch of residual sugar is often welcome. And an occasional late harvest red, with some sweetness, can be very good.

Next I want an evaluation of the acid level. The acid level makes the wine "mouth-filling" and enhances the flavors of the grape. In a white wine it feels like it cleanses the mouth. In a red wine it affects the sensors in the cheeks and creates the full, long lasting sensation that gives pleasure. We all know that long contact with the same taste or smell deadens our senses after a while-that's why women sometimes wear too much perfume: they can't smell it after the first minute or so. But a sip of wine during the meal renews our senses and allows us to continue to taste the food.

Finally, in a red wine, I'm interested in the tannins present in the wine. If it's too tannic to drink now, I want to keep it for a few years. If there's no tannin it's probably going to taste dead. And the quality of the tannins is also important-there are soft ones, and harsh ones.

Unfortunately, many of the wine writers are like a three-year-old child: they know the words, but are afraid to use them. One can only conclude from this that they feel more comfortable in being bland than in truly describing the flavors of the wine. Maybe they should switch to politics.

Eric on tractor

RANKINGS

Our friend Charles de Batz is a genuine French Baron. He is the great great great etc grandson of the famous Charles de Batz, also known as D'Artagnan, one of the three musketeers. Charles himself is a boat skipper, and-as he puts it-follows the family tradition of serving the rich.

In France introductions are more important than in the United States. Charles introduced us to his friend Eric. Eric found out we were traveling to Bordeaux, so he introduced us, by telephone, to friends of his enroute between our house in Port Grimaud, and Bordeaux. They called us and invited us to stay overnight with them and have dinner at their chateau.

During dinner, Charles' name came up, and I mentioned that he was a baron. Alexis scoffed, and explained that being a baron was nothing in France. A baron, he explained, was the lowest of the ranks of titled Frenchmen. In fact, Alexis explained, his wife Albanne is a marquise. Albanne looked down demurely. A marquis, he explained, is well above a baron, and just below a Duke! Albanne's dad took considerable time to document the fact that his ancestor fought along side General Lafayette so that he could join a special club of these descendants. Then followed a long, but interesting, explanation of every title in France and the history and significance of each one.

We thought it was pretty funny, so we told Charles about it when we returned home a few weeks later. He said he wished that he had been there to reply. The correct reply, he explained, was that while it is true that a baron is ranked lower, the title of baron is much older than the title of marquis. During the reign of King Louis whatever, there was no aristocracy in France except the barony. And therefore it's clear that only the barons are true aristocrats! In any event, he explained, he's working for a wealthy Frenchman who owns a yacht, and Alexis is working to fix up his chateau as a bed and breakfast, so the title doesn't matter that much.

I thought about this ranking of people by title while tasting Bordeaux wines at the giant Vin Expo in Bordeaux this year. Bordeaux wine is ranked a lot like Charles and Albanne. There are the Grand Crus, the First Growths, and so forth. Some of the ranking dates from 1855 and certainly must be out of date. And while the great, well known Bordeaux wines are certainly better wines than everyday inexpensive Bordeaux, I barrel tasted some wines from the next vintage of 2000 that will sell for under $30 and they were spectacular.

I know that a lot of people buy wine based on rankings. There are the Bordeaux rankings, Robert Parker's rankings, and the "Wine Spectator" rankings. The last two reduce each wine to a single number, a concept that I've never agreed with. But when there's a great vintage, like the year 2000 in Bordeaux, it pays to read some reviews, gather opinions from friends, go to a few tastings, and then buy a case or two to drink over the next few years.

VIN EXPO BORDEAUX

When I tell you that the Vin Expo held in Bordeaux France every two years is big, I mean BIG. I didn't realize how big until I discovered that it took 15 minutes for me to get, by shuttle, from the booth where my first appointment took place, to my second appointment. Every one I talked to complained that it was too big, but everyone also said they loved it and met a lot of good contacts-as I did.

It was only by chance that we ended up there. We were at our house in Port Grimaud France, when our friends from Santa Monica invited us to join them for dinner a couple of hundred miles away, in Las Rosas Spain. But why not? With the wonderful freeways in France it's not too different than driving From Santa Monica to Palm Springs for dinner.

The attraction in Las Rosas was "El Bulli," a restaurant that many of the great chefs claim has the most innovative food in the world. In fact, the chef at El Bulli only works a few months out of the year so he can travel the rest of the time tasting new foods around the world. The restaurant is situated in an old converted house on the edge of a magnificent by-out in the countryside on a road like the road to Topanga Canyon, but without the safety rails. The dinner consisted of 25 small plates of different dishes, each of which were bursting with unusual flavors. A great experience, not the least of which was an excellent bottle of a 1995 riserva from the Diurno district of Spain, made from Cabernet and Tempranillo grapes.

We knew we were going to go to Angers from Spain, to visit friends there we stay with each year. So I called into Bordeaux to get a hotel room to stay in on the way. The first 5 hotels I called said they had been booked up for over a year, since Vin Expo was under way. Finally I was lucky enough to find a room which had been reserved, but the reservation had just been canceled.

The I used the French system of calling everyone I know in France to see who they knew in Bordeaux, so I would have some new contacts while there. That was successful. Just about everyone I called knew someone with a booth a Vin Expo. And, of course, most of the producers I buy from had a booth. So we met a lot of people, new and old, made some new friends, and went to a couple of wine "soirées" put on by local producers.

Then came some invitations to stay overnight is a couple of Chateaux's that produce wine that we might buy, along with evening BBQ's with everyone in the neighborhood. Lots of fun, and lots of different wines since everyone brings with him a bottle of his latest production.

Vin Expo Bordeaux

WINE ON THE WEB

As much as I love to browse in bookstores, I'm buying more and more books off the internet. It's so convenient, and I can read reviews, other peoples' comments, and excerpts from the book all at the same time. And buying CD's is even better: I can listen to some or all of the music right from my computer before I buy!

With wine it's a bit different. Generally I can't taste it or smell it in the store, and I certainly can't with my computer, although I know a company working hard to create a device to allow smells to be generated from our computers. When that happens, buying wine on the web will have great advantages over traditional wine stores.

Wine on the web is certainly a big business. I heard that there are over a quarter of a million wine related sites on the web, and that we can buy wine from several hundreds of these sites.

One advantage is that, if you are underage and willing to perjure yourself, you can buy wine on the web, since you don't have to show any identification. A second advantage is that shopping, searching, and comparing prices is so easy on the computer. In a large wine store it's really a pain to get from the French Rhône valley area to the Italian Piedmont section, and I can never find an employee to help me. In a small wine store, where the owner is there to help, it's much better, but still lacks the facility of shopping by computer. So, if you know what you want, shopping on the computer is probably best. If you need help, shopping in a small wine store with a knowledgeable owner can't be beat. The "advice" given in the computer sites is not really very helpful, and still not interactive in real time.

What about price? That's one of the drawbacks of buying wine on the web. Books are fairly inexpensive to ship, but it costs a lot to ship wine, first because of its weight, and secondly because of the need to get it there quickly, especially during the summer months. So we have to expect to pay a bit more for wine purchased on the web, and that's most significant if we are buying inexpensive wines (as most of us do).

For a couple of other sites where I can vouch for the wine (I'm the European wine buyer for these two sites) try: www.bountyhunter-wine.com , and www.thewinebroker.com . Each of these has hard-to-find wines at reasonable prices, and knowledgeable people available on the telephone to discuss wines to fit your needs. Unlike the giant websites which are reported to be losing money on the web, these two sites are run by companies that continuously make a profit and use the web only as an adjunct to their main business. I'm also the wine buyer for www.winesamplers.com, a small company in Oregon that sells mixed cases of wine. Like many websites, this site is linked to a number of interesting international sites. Look at the "link" page for a list of these sites.

In addition to sites for buying wine on the web, there are thousands of interesting sites for gathering information about wine, wine related areas and wine products. Many of the famous French Chateaux have their own websites, such as www.beychevelle.com ,(visit the chateau!) www.latourfigeac.com and www.smith-haut-lafitte.com .

There are, of course, hundreds of private merchants selling on the web, such as The Chicago Wine company (an auction bidding site) at www.tcwc.com and the Oregon Pinot Noir Club (www.oregonpinot-noir.com).

For me, one of the most valuable uses of the web is to search promotional sites of a particular region. Almost every major wine region has its own site, and many are loaded with interesting information. Here are a few:

Australian Wine Bureau
www.wineaustralia.com

Wines of Austria
www.austrian.wine.co.at

Conseil Interprofessionnel du Vin de Bordeaux
www.vins-bordeaux.fr

Italian Trade Centre
www.italianwineguide.com

Wine Institute of New Zealand
www.nzwine.com

Port Wine Institute
www.ivp.pt (a beautiful site)

Wines of California
www.winesofcalifornia.com

I can't wait for that new smell box to be available so we can smell the wine on the web before we buy!

April 23, 2001

THE ROYAL CASTLE OF VERDUNO

The home of Barolo

We love Italy. Italy is a young nation, and Italians think of themselves as residents of their region, more than as "Italians." The region we like the best to visit is the North-West of Italy called the Piedmonte, or "foothills." It is famous for truffles, mushrooms, hazelnuts, and wines from the Nebbiolo, Dolcetto, and Barbera grapes. And within the Piemonte region, we like the area around the town of Alba, especially the Royal castle at Verduno.

In 1847, King Carlo Alberto of Savoy, the father of Vittorio Emanuelle II—the first King of Italy, tasted the wines of this castle, and loved them so much-he bought the entire estate! In the early 1900's it was purchased by Sr. Burlotto, who left it to his three daughters. They turned it into a thirteen room rustic hotel. One daughter runs the hotel, one runs the kitchen, and the third-Gabriella-married the son of Luigi Bianco ("white Louis") from the neighboring town of Barbaresco. Luigi, and his adjacent neighbor Angelo Gaja, have been the cornerstones of winemaking in Barbaresco.

Today the Castello di Verduno is a wonderful place to visit and spend a few days, particularly in October during the truffle festival in Alba, just a few miles away. Turin, the largest city in the area, (and the birth-place of ice cream) is also very close, and is very beautiful. But the most interesting parts of the Piedmont for me are the numerous small villages, each with its own personality and individual sites and history. Some are home to a famous regional restaurant. Many have small churches of great beauty, and sometimes historical significance. At least two villages have historic, preserved synagogues from the time when the Jews were prominent in this region. Many villages have food and wine festivals, and some have festivals celebrating some important event in history.

With the techniques learned in Barbaresco and the grapes and cellars of Verduno, Franco Bianco and Gabriella Burlotto continued the

234

tradition of making the fine wines of Verduno. Today they make Barolo, Barbaresco, Docetto, Nebbiolo, Barbara, and Pelevarga, a varietal grown only at Verduno. Each year hundreds of German wine lovers descend on Verduno at harvest time to load up their cars with the new vintages. What little remains is sold to Fourcade & Hecht wines of California. You can savor a glass of the Verduno Dolcetto d'Alba at a number of fine restaurants in this area, including Dante's in Pacific Palisades, and I Cugini in Santa Monica.

Gabriella Burlotto and Franco Bianco, winemakers

DIFFICULT QUESTIONS

Conventional wisdom says that when two American men meet for the first time and strike up a conversation, the initial topics are likely to be sports and weather. If two Chinese men meet in the same situation, one is likely to ask the other "how much money did you make last year?"

While sailing in the San Blas Islands off the coast of Panama one year, I struck up a conversation with a Cuna Indian gentleman. His first question went like this: "You know, we sleep in hammocks. Once I saw a western bed like you sleep in. Tell me, how do you folks make love on such a flat space?"

I thought about those questions while reading a February wine column by Frank Prial in the New York Times, as he describes difficult questions he is asked, such as: "what is your favorite wine," and "what is your favorite wine experience." He says he has problems answering those questions.

I have no problem at all with those questions. I recall vividly the first time we ordered a really expensive bottle of Bordeaux. I was about to graduate from Law School. We went to Lockober's, the best restaurant in Boston. We couldn't sit in the grill room, because in those days it was "men only." [How times have changed!] So we sat in the grand dining room and ordered a bottle of Lafite Rothschild. I remember thinking that it went extremely well with the roast beef, just as well as Pepsi Cola did with pizza, my usual dinner fare. Twenty years later I had another bottle of the same wine, but a later vintage, with friends at a restaurant in Venice that is no longer there, in the old Bank of America building. And I remember thinking it was like drinking the essence of violets. And it brought back memories of Lockober's.

Then Bonnie got her first Master's degree, and we went to Europe. In Paris we drank a glass of Chateau d'Yquem Sauternes, the best sweet white wine made in the world (then and now). The only souvenir we brought back with us was a bottle of Chateau d'Yquem. In 1991 I opened my last bottle of 1971 Barolo that I had carefully preserved in my cellar. It was at a family dinner, during which I was pontificating on the wonders of Italian wine. As I poured the wine we all noticed that it was the color of light rosé. As I continued to pour, suddenly the room smelled like a rose garden. When we tasted the wine, it had a slight sweetness, a heady floral nose, and an intense fruit flavor. Then I knew what it meant to properly age a fine wine.

In 1995 our close friends took us for a picnic at the Ridge Winery near Redwood City California. They brought the finest delicacies, and all of my favorite cold things to eat. We bought a few bottles of wine from the winery, and sat at the picnic tables. I think Ridge Zinfandel is wonderful, year after year, and when I drink it I think of that picnic.

Each of these wines is my favorite, and each of these experiences is the best I ever had. After almost every meal my dad used to say "that was the best meal I ever ate." And so it seems.

As to the difficult questions: for the Chinese gentleman, my answer is "Gross or net?" For my Cuna friend, you can answer that as well as I.

Sailing Freedom in the San Blas Islands

RECIPE INDEX